It's Not *Just* About The Money

It's Not *Just* About The Money

The Whole-Life Approach to Wealth Management

SUSAN LATREMOILLE

L
G P

Latremoille Group Publishing

FIRST EDITION
Susan Latremoille
181 Bay St., Suite 3910
Toronto, ON M5J 2T3
Phone: 416-969-3026
Email: info@TheLatremoilleGroup.com
www.TheLatremoilleGroup.com

Library and Archives Canada Cataloguing in Publication

Latremoille, Susan, 1951-
It's not just about the money : the whole-life approach to wealth management / Susan Latremoille.

ISBN 978-0-9781401-3-7

1. Wealth--Management. 2. Rich people--Finance, Personal. 3. Finance, Personal. 4. Investments. I. Title.

HG179.L369 2010 332.024'01 C2010-905457-1

PRINTED IN CANADA
Book Cover & Text Design: Angel Guerra/Archetype
Author Photograph: Horst Herget

To my loyal clients – it is an honour knowing that you entrust the management of your wealth to me.

Contents

Preface

My first book, *The RichLife*, tells the story of where I come from and how I came to be the person I am today. Some have called it a memoir, and I guess in some ways that is what it is.

It describes my grandfather's life as an important banker in Prague and my grandmother's life and her many roles. She was a homemaker par excellence, raising a young family and managing a large household with many servants; she was the ultimate corporate wife, organizing the lavish entertainments my grandfather's position required; she was a pillar of society and a very hands-on patron of promising young artists.

The RichLife also tells the story of my family's sudden change of circumstances: my father was a Jew, and the rise of the Nazi regime forced him to abandon his home and flee to safety with his family, first to Holland and then to England. Although the war destroyed many things, it never destroyed his optimism and vision.

From England my father moved to Ontario where he had bought a farm, which is where he started to rebuild his life. In Canada he met and married my mother. If my father was the visionary, my mother was the practical partner who made things work—she was the one with the business sense, and it was her guidance that made his ideas bear fruit. My father kindled in me the fires of his passion, values, and vision. My mother taught me that organization and determination are a powerful combination when it comes to accomplishing goals. *The RichLife* was all about how my parents and their example forged my character and my perspective on the world.

Many of my clients have read that book, and many have given me very similar feedback on it. They said the book gives a good impression of who I am on a personal level and shows my very real concern for my clients' overall well-being but seems to be missing something important.

"Susan, it shows the soft side of what you do," one of them told me, "but it doesn't give the reader a clue about how you manage money so effectively. It doesn't say anything about the nitty-gritty of how you have structured your practice."

The present book, then, attempts to redress that imbalance. It focuses more closely on the disciplines and processes that characterize my unique approach to managing my clients' wealth.

My approach to investment management is holistic. I do not use this term in some vague, New Age sense but in the true sense of the word: I believe the whole of every human being is bigger than the sum of his or her parts. I think of my approach as a whole-life approach, and I mean that in two ways: it considers priorities in every aspect of my clients' lives, and it is based on the anticipation of a lifelong advisory relationship.

In my practice, as in most, it is understood that preservation and growth of capital constitute the first priority; the difference is that my clients know exactly what they are preserving and growing their capital for. This book explains how they come to articulate a clear vision of their life goals and how that vision affects the appropriate investment of their assets. My work is about money, of course, but as you will see, it is not just about the money.

You will meet some of my clients as you read this book. Their stories are based on actual experiences and interactions, and they are presented here as composites to illustrate certain issues and how those issues were resolved. Their names and some details of their stories have been changed to protect their privacy.

I hope this book will be worth the time you devote to reading it. I hope it will be the catalyst you need to develop a fuller vision of what your wealth can do for you. That it will lead you to a better relationship with your own advisor—or at the very least make you aware of what you may reasonably expect a dedicated financial advisor's services to include. Nothing would please me more than for my book to do its part in encouraging frank conversations about the client-advisor relationship, making that relationship richer and fuller, and making lives richer and fuller as a result. It will certainly give you some pointers on how to interview advisors if you do not currently have one or feel you need to switch.

This book will show you how effective a complex process can be when it is organized into individual steps. Best of all, it may get you to think in a new way about what you want your wealth to achieve for you and the steps you can take to get there.

Before we begin, let me share this quotation by W. Somerset Maugham that has inspired me in my life:

> *It's a funny thing about life;*
> *if you refuse to accept anything but the best,*
> *you very often get it.*

Introduction

Whenever I start to read a new book, I feel I am embarking on a journey. Just as when I'm actually traveling to a new place, I become filled with excitement and anticipation, hoping the journey will live up to my expectations. One thing that's true of any type of journey is that it usually helps to have a map at hand. This brief introduction is intended to be your map.

You are about to read a book about wealth management. Although in the final analysis the book must stand on its own merits as you judge them, I have assumed that you would like to know a bit about the person who wrote the book before you fully commit to a trip with her. Therefore the first chapter provides a synopsis of my twenty-five-year career in the investment industry. It explains my philosophy of wealth management and describes the structures I have put in place to ensure that this philosophy comes to life for the benefit of my clients in the work I do.

Chapters 2 through 4 are about the investment industry and investment success. In them you will find a brief history of the industry in Canada and a discussion of the differences between various types of investment professionals. You will also learn about the specific processes and strategies I have developed to help my clients articulate and achieve both their financial and their non-financial goals. If you are self-managing your investments or considering doing so, you will be particularly interested in the discussion of the characteristics that are essential for success.

Business owners may find Chapter 5 especially interesting because it highlights issues they face and unique solutions I can bring through a network of specialists in many areas, including corporate finance, tax planning, estate planning, philanthropy, investment planning, insurance planning and family dynamics.

In my practice over the years, I have come to realize that there are certain characteristics that limit people's comfort with the investment process. Chapter 6 explores such characteristics that can arise among certain women clients and discusses ways in which we work with them to increase their knowledge about investing and their comfort with the process.

Family money and its transition from one generation to another can be a blessing or a curse. Chapter 7 discusses both sides of this reality.

No book on investing would be complete without a discussion of retirement. Is there enough money? When should I retire? What will I do? Should I consider not retiring? These are among the questions considered in chapter 8.

Chapter 9 discusses the characteristics of a good investment advisor and gives specific tips on how to interview a prospective advisor to ensure that you choose the right one: someone who acts with your best interests in mind and who structures their practice to provide the level of service you require.

The book ends with chapter 10, Last Words. In it, you will get a glimpse of the specialized resources available to me through my firm, and more to the point, the benefits that these resources bring to my clients.

I hope you find this map a helpful start to your reading, and I trust you will find the book itself a helpful guide to success in both your financial and personal endeavours.

Susan Latremoille, *July 2010*

Chapter 1

The Latremoille Group Philosophy

Money: Wonderful Servant, Heartless Master

Twenty-five years of experience have taught me how to manage money effectively. Those years have also taught me an invaluable related skill: how to help my clients use their money in ways that make it more likely they will achieve their important non-financial goals.

I have guided my clients through all the major market "disasters" of the last quarter century, including the unprecedented crash of 1987, when the Dow dropped more than 22% in one day—its largest one-day decline since hostilities were initiated in World War I; the savings & loan crisis of 1997, when more than two thousand U.S. banks and Savings & Loans went bankrupt; the bursting of the tech bubble in 2000 and the resulting chaos in the markets; and the most recent carnage from late 2008 to early 2009, created by the subprime debacle and ensuing credit crisis that saw once-venerable firms like Merrill Lynch, Bear Stearns, and Lehman Brothers fold for good. On any long-term chart, these disasters are mere blips in a market that has consistently moved to new highs over time.

Through these tough times, and through the thankfully much longer and more rewarding good times, I have paid very close attention both to the markets and my clients. My philosophy of business, which combines responsible wealth management with an absolute commitment to extensive, individualized client service, grew out of this focused observation.

In my approach, your wealth is your whole life. Notice I did not say your money is your whole life. In my view, wealth is not just the money you have; it is the life you have, supported by your money. So in a very real sense, wealth management is life management. But don't get me wrong here: I am not a life coach. I am first and foremost a wealth advisor to individuals and families who have worked hard enough, worked smart enough, and been fortunate enough to establish a comfortable level of affluence. My first responsibility—and always my first priority—is the preservation and growth of my clients' assets.

Over the years, though, I have seen that there are basically two types of clients: those who are in control of their money and those who are controlled by their money. What is the biggest difference between these clients? Their attitude toward their money.

For both groups money is important, but for different reasons. Just as I do, the first group views money as an enabler, a resource for accomplishing their clearly articulated life goals; the second group sees money as an end in itself, and their primary goal in life is to accumulate more of it. Both groups are wealthy; you can probably guess which is happier.

The Whole-Life Approach to Wealth Management

As my philosophy has developed over the years, I have taken lessons from both groups of clients, and I have designed my practice to implement the lessons learned from the first group. I take a whole-life approach to wealth management, and as I indicated in the preface to this book, it is a whole-life approach in two ways.

First, it takes into consideration the decisions you make about what you want from every aspect of your life—your work or your activities in retirement, your relationships with family and friends, your lifestyle, your concern about your community, your wishes about how your assets will be disbursed after you die—and it brings those decisions to bear on how your money is invested now and how you use it.

Second, it is based on my expectation, when I accept a new client, that I will work on that client's behalf in a relationship that spans the client's natural life and/or the rest of my professional life, and this includes putting in place plans to ensure that the client's wishes are fulfilled posthumously.

In later chapters, you will see some of the techniques I use to help my clients articulate their goals, both financial and non-financial—goals that to me are intricately intertwined. Please keep in mind as you read that a thorough understanding of my clients' non-financial goals is the foundation I need for ensuring that their financial affairs are organized in the optimal manner.

When I said above that I have designed my practice based on lessons learned from those who use their money as an enabler, I meant exactly that. I have consciously designed every element of the way I do business.

For example, I have moved from one firm to another twice in my career, from Merrill Lynch Canada to RBC Dominion Securities in 1990 and from that firm to Richardson Partners Financial Limited fourteen years later, both times to accomplish specific objectives.

For more than seven years I worked in the Institutional Equity Sales group at Merrill Lynch, where all of my clients were professional money managers, such as pension funds, mutual fund companies, banks, and insurance companies. For five of those years I specialized in the U.S. equity market. I worked with one hundred Wall Street analysts who covered all of the various industries, learning how professionals make investment decisions. It was an invaluable training ground.

But I often asked myself what I was training for. I was successful, but not satisfied. I felt the work I was doing, while comfortably remunerative, made no discernible difference. Then, through a series of conversations over many months with my mentor, my friends and family members, and my colleagues, I decided I could put the knowledge I had gained to better use by helping individuals rather than big institutions meet their investment objectives. That decision marked a turning point in my career: my move from the institutional side of the business to the private client side.

Having researched my options, I decided RBC Dominion Securities offered the fullest and deepest complement of financial capabilities and services available, and in 1990 I joined that firm's Private Client Division and began advising private clients. As I had expected, my time in training really did position me well for this change, and also as I had expected I found the work much more fulfilling. In 1995 I was appointed a vice president of RBC Dominion Securities and a member of their Private Client Advisory Board.

As my clients became more affluent, and as I began to attract clients who were more affluent to begin with, I realized that I could not continue on my own to provide the standard of client service that was largely responsible for my success and that my clients had every right to expect. In 1994, in spite of hard times and against the advice of others, I decided to build a team at RBC Dominion to better serve my clients. I hired two young women to assist me, and both are with me still (though they are not quite as young now). You will learn more about how my expanded team operates a bit further on in this chapter.

Fast-forward ten years. We had weathered the S&L crisis and the tech meltdown. The investment landscape had changed dramatically. There were now innumerable investment products that had not existed a decade earlier, many of them far too complex for even some financial advisors to understand. My clientele had also changed. I was now dealing almost exclusively with very wealthy people, and I realized that my clients' needs were different from what they had been in the mid-1990's. Even with a dedicated, professional team in place, I felt my clients deserved more than I could deliver through my firm.

• • •

Again I undertook thorough research of investment firms, and one stood out far above the crowd. This firm had been founded by the Richardsons, an extremely successful entrepreneurial family. Frustrated by the lack of specialized financial services available to meet their investment and planning needs, they took their customary approach and figured it out for themselves so other highly successful individuals and families with similar needs could benefit from what they had learned. They founded Richardson Partners Financial Limited in 2003.

This firm, however, did not materialize out of nothing—it grew out of their experience in commodities trading. Early in the last century the Richardsons began to offer advice and brokerage services to grain farmers, who speculated with some of the money they got for their crops. So the family had solid investment experience when in 1926 they founded Richardson Securities, which became Richardson Greenshields, which in turn was bought by the Royal Bank of Canada in 1996.

At any rate, I moved to Richardson Partners Financial Limited (now Richardson GMP) as a partner in 2004, feeling I had finally found the working environment in which my philosophy of wealth management could be fully realized. I have not been disappointed; nor have my clients.

Let's take a closer look at exactly what my philosophy entails.

The Latremoille Group Philosophy in Action

One simple, declarative sentence expresses the philosophical foundation of my approach to wealth management: Life is about more than money. This foundation supports four elements that transform what could be a merely philosophical perspective into a practical, applied system of investment management: Vision, Commitment, Support, and Simplification. Let me say more about these elements.

• • •

Transforming Vision into Vital Reality. In my practice, we invest in our clients, not just for them. We work with them to understand their broader vision of their lives because the vision they have for the future influences the way their assets should be invested today.

Some people are very clear about what they want from life. They know what is important to them, and they articulate and prioritize goals as a way of guiding their current actions. Many of them have taken the time to write down detailed three- or five-year plans as well as much longer-term blueprints. Our work with this group is fairly straightforward. We get to know them, get to understand their goals, and agree on how their assets should be invested to meet those goals.

Other people are less clear about what they want. They take a kind of path-of-least-resistance approach to life, and the unfortunate result is that they are buffeted about by chance occurrences. We work with this group to help them articulate their vision by deciding what is most important to them in every aspect of their lives. Once they have decided what they want from life, we proceed with the investment of assets. The techniques we have developed to help clients articulate their vision are discussed in later chapters.

With every one of our clients, our objective is to ensure that all of their resources are in the right place so they can realize their vision as a living reality now and in the future.

If you have been reading between the lines, you have already concluded that my approach requires a real relationship with my clients. Which leads us to the second element of my philosophy.

Our Commitment to Your Prosperity and Peace of Mind. Commitment is more than a buzzword to the Latremoille Group; it is a cornerstone of the way we operate. In the processes we use to manage wealth and in the structure of our team, we are completely committed to your prosperity and to your peace of mind. That is why we limit the number of clients we accept. Nothing demonstrates our commitment better than this purposeful restriction of our client base and the way our team works with the clients we do accept. We have one of the highest staff-to-client ratios of any investment team in Canada, and the team is structured to deliver uncommon service.

Appropriate investment of assets is the starting point in ensuring your ongoing prosperity. We also ensure your peace of mind by keeping informed about your investments. We provide regular communication tailored to your preferences—that is, with the frequency you request and in a reporting format you determine. In addition, because of the way our team operates, our clients can always reach us for answers to any questions they may have about any aspect of their affairs.

Supporting Our Clients in Uncommon Ways and Simplifying Their Lives. We believe it is important for both the client and the advisor to feel that they have found the right fit. "Chemistry" is therefore one of the factors we consider when deciding whether to accept a new client. Every member of our team knows our clients and every client knows our team. Because we do restrict the number of clients, and because each of our team members has specialized functions, we are able to keep on top of client affairs in extraordinary ways. Let me relate a client story to illustrate my point.

In 2008 a couple who had had their assets at an investment counseling firm for more than twenty years—mostly because the woman's cousin was a principal in the firm—moved their assets to us when the cousin died.

As you may know, investment counselors generally maintain certain model portfolios: one for aggressive clients who are willing to accept substantial risk in the hope of higher returns, one for conservative clients who are risk averse, and others for the clients in between who can tolerate modest amounts of risk in order to meet their goals.

When these investment counselors take on a new client, they manage the client's money by channeling it into one of these model portfolios, either in pooled funds or in segregated accounts, just like the money of other clients of the same risk profile. In other words, every one of their clients within a risk profile has essentially the same portfolio. Fair enough—investment counselors are quite straightforward about what they offer. But this is obviously not the right approach for someone who requires customized attention.

We contacted this couple's tax accountant as part of our review of their affairs. We discovered that although the investment counselors had taken losses each year in the investment pool, they had not tailored their tax-loss selling to the couple's particular circumstances; nor had they reviewed their individual tax situation retroactively. Again, this is simply not part of how they operate.

One of my team members is responsible for maintaining contact with clients' tax advisors so we are aware of their tax situation on a continuing basis. You may remember that 2005, 2006, and 2007 were very strong investment years; many people realized substantial capital gains during that period. When planning tax-loss selling, if you look at just the current year you can miss opportunities to offset gains from previous years. Fortunately, with the additional information the accountant provided about the couple's situation we were able to offset previous years' gains through strategic tax-loss selling.

There is another element in our approach to our clients' tax situation that sets us apart from most money managers and investment advisors: we start our selling in September, not in December. Here is why. By being proactive, by looking at a client's realized gains and losses to date and also at those that are unrealized, and with the information from the client's tax advisors, we have a thorough understanding of their tax situation. Once we get a fix on that we start doing the tax-loss selling in September and we buy back. If the market declines before December, or if individual securities have lost value, there is another opportunity to sell. We know what gains the client has realized and therefore we know how much of their losses can be reported on their tax return to reduce the tax they would otherwise have to pay on their gains.

The results of this approach are tangible: in 2008, for example, most of our clients received substantial tax refunds, and only because we were on it early, monitoring their tax situations closely during the last four months of the year.

This is standard practice for us—for every client, every year. It is part of our commitment to client service and to our clients' ongoing prosperity. It is also part of our commitment to simplifying our clients' lives: we take care of the many necessary details of their investment affairs, details that would otherwise require their time and effort to administer.

My product is advice, and as you will see in coming chapters, I make every effort to ensure that my clients receive the best possible advice about their affairs. Knowing they can rely on advice that takes full account of both their financial and non-financial goals is a major source of peace of mind for them. Knowing they can also count on continuing to receive this kind of advice is another. They know this because they know that as I have built and developed my team I have also been developing a sound succession plan.

My team members are not simply "support staff"; they are investment professionals in their own right. Among our team members are people who have achieved designation as portfolio managers and people who are licensed in insurance. In addition, our team brings a depth of experience and level of stability that is rare in our industry—two of my team members have been with me for more than sixteen years! All team members are thoroughly familiar with the processes I have put in place to serve our clients' needs; in fact, on a day-to-day basis it is they who ensure that this process runs smoothly. Our clients know if I were hit by that proverbial bus tomorrow, they could rely on my team for expert advice and for seamless administration of their affairs.

Chapter 2

What Every Client Should Know:

Investment Advisors, the Investment Process, and the Investment Industry

My dentist always has the radio on in her office, and it's usually playing soothing classical music; I guess she's trying to put people at ease. On my last visit, though, I happened to be in the chair during a newsbreak. The stories were mostly about world and national events—war and politics, as one of my friends says—but one of the items covered in the program was the recent call for more regulation of the investment industry.

"I'm all for that," my dentist said. "After all, what layperson can possibly understand what their advisor recommends?"

With dental instruments in my mouth, I could hardly respond, but it got me thinking. Here was a successful medical professional in mid-career, making well over $200,000 a year, yet she was admitting with that brief question that she didn't really know much about how the investment industry operates or about how her advisor manages her money.

From my point of view, that's a bad situation. I believe anyone who has money to invest has the right, perhaps even the obligation, to understand how their money is invested. Otherwise, how can they have peace of mind?

A Whirlwind History of the Investment Industry

I have always believed you can't understand something thoroughly until you understand its history. So to appreciate the lay of the land in today's investment industry, it may be useful to take a quick, high-level look at how it has changed over the past twenty-five or thirty years. Don't worry, I'm not about to launch into a doctoral dissertation on the industry and all the minute changes that have occurred; I just want to paint a picture in broad strokes—a kind of impressionist view that highlights the big events.

In the not too distant past, that is, until the 1980s, the financial industry in Canada was highly stratified. There were four distinct types of financial institutions: banks, trust companies, insurance companies, and investment firms. These companies were so distinct, in fact, that they were referred to as the four pillars of the financial industry, and they operated as separate silos. No company in any one of these pillars could own a company in another, nor could it offer the products or services of another. For example, banks could not own trust companies or insurance companies or investment dealers; they could not provide trust services or insurance coverage through their own operations; and their investment products were limited primarily to the deposit vehicles they offered, mostly GICs and term deposits.

Then the 1980s ushered in an era of deregulation that eventually dismantled the regulatory strictures that had kept these pillars separate for so long. Banks bought trust companies and investment dealers. The personnel of both could get insurance licences. Investment dealers who remained independent of banks could also provide insurance coverage and banking services.

Some decried this amalgamation of financial services as an abandonment of tradition, a dangerous move away from a proven, conservative financial system. Others welcomed it as a move toward greater competition and a freer marketplace, and they speculated that the consumer of financial services would be the real winner.

Whichever view one took, the result of all that change was the Canadian financial industry as we know it today. Deregulated? Yes. Unregulated? Hardly!

In fact, the regulations currently in place in the Canadian financial industry are largely responsible for the stability our banking system demonstrated in the aftermath of the 2008/2009 subprime meltdown and the ensuing credit crisis. As well, firms in the Canadian investment industry are governed by the rules and regulations of the Investment Industry Regulatory Organization of Canada (IIROC); these cover everything from administrative practices to capital requirements to trading practices and ethical standards of conduct for employees.

I know from direct experience how seriously regulators monitor the conduct of investment professionals. After winning the Award of Distinction from the Investment Dealers Association of Canada (IDA, precursor to the IROC), I served a term as the industry representative on the association's three-member Disciplinary Committee, where my co-committee members were an IDA representative and a judge.

As part of its effort to ensure that advisors have the knowledge they need to stay current with new products and practices in a rapidly changing industry, IIROC has instituted mandatory continuing education requirements for those who give investment advice to private investors. Operating on three-year cycles, the continuing education program requires advisors to complete a Compliance course and a Professional Development course during each cycle.

Does this mean nothing can ever go wrong? No, of course not. But it does mean firms are held to a high standard, and every firm has a compliance department devoted to ensuring that all regulatory requirements are met. So yes, the financial industry was deregulated a quarter-century ago, but today's environment cannot accurately be characterized as unregulated.

Brokers and Planners and Counselors! Oh, My!

Dorothy and her friends were understandably concerned when they chanted, "Lions and tigers and bears! Oh, my!" They were frightened at the prospect of meeting one or more of those wild creatures as they followed the Yellow Brick Road through the forest to the Emerald City. But at least they knew what each of those animals was. This gives them an advantage over many investors today: one of the realities investors face is the daunting task of choosing an investment professional. And because advisors call themselves different things—broker, planner, counselor, to name a few—it is sometimes difficult to understand exactly what they are, what models they operate under, and what services they offer. Let's try to get some clarity on these issues.

Investors have different needs. They have different goals when it comes to their investments. And they have different amounts of investible assets. All of these factors come to bear in finding an investment advisor. It's important to find the advisor who is right for you: that is, one whose services offer the best match with your needs, your goals, and your assets. So let's take a few minutes to try to highlight some of the differences between the various types of professionals who offer investment advice.

Stockbrokers. Back in the days before deregulation, most investment firms were referred to as brokerage houses and most advisors who dealt with individual investors were called stockbrokers. As the word broker implies, they functioned as a go-between: basically as someone who brokered deals between their clients and the capital markets. Investors could not purchase stocks and bonds directly, as they can nowadays with online trading, so if they wanted to invest in the capital markets they had to go through someone who was licensed to purchase and sell investment securities. That someone was a stockbroker, and stockbrokers got paid by receiving a commission on each purchase and sale they completed on behalf of a client. Many advisors, whether they call themselves brokers or not, still use this payment model today.

The advice brokers offered was primarily which securities to buy or sell and when to do so. They had an obligation to follow the Know

Your Client rule, as all advisors still do today. Industry regulators put this rule in place to help ensure that advisors give appropriate investment advice to a client. For many, however, the extent to which they needed to know their client was generally understood as the need to determine the client's financial situation and how each of the following goals figured in the client's overall investment objectives: preservation of capital, growth of capital, and income from investments. They also needed to assess how much risk the client could tolerate, and brokers were expected to recommend only securities that were in line with a client's objectives and tolerance for risk.

Financial Planners. By the early 1980s, another model of advice had emerged: the financial planning model. Financial planning was still based on the Know Your Client rule, but planners interpreted that rule more broadly—or perhaps I should say more deeply. In addition to understanding the investment objectives and risk tolerance noted above, they incorporated retirement planning, tax planning, and estate planning into their service offering, and they helped clients plan how to fund their children's or grandchildren's education.

Two types of financial planner emerged.

The first type of financial planner prepares financial plans for a fee but does not sell any type of investment product to the client.

The second type does not charge for financial plans but does sell investment products to the client.

The rise of the latter type of financial planning coincided, not surprisingly, with a burgeoning of the mutual fund industry. I say not surprisingly because the product offering of most financial planners was confined to mutual funds of the company they worked for. And the payment model was trailer fees—that is, fees that the fund company paid to those who sold the funds, based on the cost of the funds to the client. Over the years, the commission structure became more complex (with front-end load and back-end load funds and fees for early redemption, for example), and many new types of funds came into being: open-end funds, closed-end funds, index funds, exchange-traded funds, and funds of funds, to name just a few.

Financial planners did what their name implies, and they offered a more comprehensive financial plan than brokers, to be sure. I call that a real, tangible service to the investing public. It was a much-needed service that previously had been available only to the very wealthy and now was available to anyone who had even a modest nest egg of assets to invest.

Investment Counselors. Speaking of the very wealthy brings us to a discussion of investment counselors. Investment counselors cater to the investment needs of wealthy individual investors and of large institutions such as banks, insurance companies, and pension funds. They, too, help clients figure out their objectives, and then, as mentioned above, invest the client's money in one of several model portfolios, either in large investment pools or in segregated accounts that the counselors manage.

That is to say, if a client's profile is that of an extremely conservative investor, then that client's money goes into the most conservative portfolio, which will be composed mainly of high-grade bonds. If a client is able to tolerate a high degree of risk in the hope of achieving higher returns, then that client's assets go into the portfolio of aggressive growth equities. And if the client is somewhere between these extremes, i.e., able to tolerate moderate risk in return for somewhat greater returns, then that client's money goes into the balanced portfolio, generally composed of a mix of bonds and blue chip stocks.

In other words, as discussed earlier, every conservative investor has the same portfolio, every aggressive investor has the same portfolio, and every moderate investor has the same portfolio. Some investment counselors also had access to alternative securities, such as real estate and hedge funds, that have not generally been available to clients through other advisors until more recently. Initially these investments were available to the counselors through third parties; now, however, many investment counselors offer them directly. Alternative securities are not appropriate for all clients. As an advisor to the wealthy, I use them only when they are a suitable option and serve a specific purpose in an individual client's portfolio.

The primary benefit of this approach is its efficiency as a way to achieve active management of large sums of money. The payment model for investment counselors is generally a percentage of assets under management rather than a commission on purchases and sales. This percentage is usually calculated on a sliding scale: for example, a certain percent on the first $500,000, a somewhat smaller percent on the next $250,000, and so on.

Many investors find this a very attractive payment option because it completely sidesteps the lingering concern about commission-based advisors: that their buy or sell recommendations may be motivated by their own interests more than their clients' interests—after all, it is only through transacting business for their clients that they get paid. Investors should be aware, though, that they are also paying management and custody fees, and sometimes commissions that are not included in the basic percent-of-assets fee.

A Little Secret About Assessing Investment Goals

You have probably noticed by now that the starting point for all advisors is the assessment of their clients' investment goals and risk tolerance. Such an assessment forms the basis for decisions about asset allocation in a client's portfolio and about the specific securities that will comprise the portfolio. Some are more thorough in this assessment than others, but the well-kept little secret is that the process for determining investment goals and asset allocation is pretty much the same from advisor to advisor and from firm to firm.

Does the client want preservation of capital or growth of capital or some combination of the two? What are the client's needs for income from their investments? How much risk is the client willing to take in order to meet their investment goals? These are the immediate considerations that must be taken into account when deciding asset allocation. Thanks to the influence of the financial planning sector, most assessment processes now also include retirement planning and education planning.

So, if the models for assessing investment goals get everyone pretty much to the same starting point, what actually differentiates one advisor from another? Well, as we've seen, there are differences in how advisors receive their remuneration. As we've also seen, there are some differences in the investment products available to different advisors. And we've seen that some investment services are available only through certain advisors.

But wait a minute. Is the question that starts the last paragraph the right question to be asking? It is true that every advisor needs certain basic information from a client in order to invest the client's money responsibly. But even though all assessment models are designed to get at least this basic information, does that mean all advisors start from pretty much the same point? The answer is a definitive no. Why? Because some models are designed to get much more than the bare minimum of information.

In the final analysis, the real differentiator is how successful an advisor is in understanding each client's unique circumstances, and how effective the advisor is in translating those circumstances into a cohesive, comprehensive, whole-life wealth strategy. Such effectiveness assumes the advisor brings the right qualifications to their work, and it presupposes a client-service model that is not simply responsive but rather proactive in meeting the specific needs and desires of each client.

The next chapter highlights some of the strategies I use to make sure I really know each of my clients as a unique individual with unique needs before I begin to formulate ideas about how their money should be invested.

Chapter 3

Owning Your Financial Success

We have just seen that the investment process itself is similar from advisor to advisor; after all, there are only so many ways an advisor can present recommendations on asset allocation and security selection. There is a very great difference, however, in the amount of information different advisors consider adequate, the techniques they use to get this information, and the ways they use the information they get.

It's one thing to determine a client's age, marital status, income, net worth, investible assets, financial goals, and risk tolerance—the bare minimum of information industry regulators require to satisfy the Know Your Client rule. It is quite another to understand what a client considers most important in life and to appreciate what that client's priorities are in order to design an investment plan that benefits the client in every aspect of their life. I am completely committed to the latter approach.

The R-Factor: Asking the Right Questions

I believe it is important to have an in-depth, structured conversation before even thinking about the structure of a client's portfolio. In a sense, getting the right information is a matter of asking the right questions—and sometimes it is also a matter of helping people answer them. If the numbers—age, income, net worth, etc.—are the bare bones, then answers to the right questions put flesh on the bones. The right questions are the ones that change someone from a prospect into a person. In other words, asking these questions is the point at which routine ends and relationship begins.

In my quest for the right questions—questions that can guide a conversation in beneficial directions—I am forever indebted to Dan Sullivan of The Strategic Coach®, who introduced me to what he calls the R-Factor Question®. This question is designed to help people articulate what is most important in their future and reveal the scope of their goals. It helps people formulate the goals they want to have accomplished three years in the future. In my practice, I use both the R-Factor Question® that Dan created as well as a modified R-Factor Question® with a much longer timeframe.

Zooming out, I usually ask the modified question first: "If you were at the end of your life looking back to today, what would have to have happened in the interim for you to feel you've lived your life with no regrets?"

The first response I often get is something like, "Wow, that's a big question." And that is an absolutely appropriate response—it is a big question. Part of the power of the question lies in the fact that it broadens people's focus: it seems to release them from their current, everyday concerns and remind them of what has special, lasting importance to them.

It is a question that gets people thinking really long-term about what they want to accomplish in their lives. Some people answer right away; they are the goal-oriented ones who have the written three- or five-year plans in their top drawers. Some take time to consider the question before answering. Still others seem stymied by the enormousness of the question; it often helps them if we ask them what would have to happen for them to have no regrets in specific areas of their lives. Some people prefer answering this question in a later meeting, after they have had time to think it through on their own.

Whichever of these categories clients fit into, their answers always include their financial goals. Not surprisingly, though, given the scope of the question, their answers almost always go beyond the financial to include their thoughts about such things as their health, their relationships with family and friends, their career aspirations, how they want to live in retirement, any philanthropic goals they may have, and the mark they want to leave when they are gone. This is not an exhaustive list, but these are among the most frequent responses I get. These responses reflect how people see themselves; in essence, they say a lot about how they want to be in the world and how they want to be remembered. They remind people of what they are most passionate about.

Zooming back in, I follow this modified question with the R-Factor Question® itself: "Three years from now, what would have to have happened for you to look back and be happy about your progress?" With its relatively short three-year timeframe, this question helps people focus on more immediate concerns. If the first question is about being, this second question is about doing: it usually elicits answers that have to do with what people think they need to accomplish to make significant progress toward their more encompassing life goals.

You may be reading this and thinking, "Why is it necessary for an investment professional to know all these personal details about a client's life?" The short answer is that it is not necessary. Not all advisors seek this level of information. So I can only answer why it is necessary for me.

Which takes us back to the R-Factor Questions. The "R" in the name stands for Relationship, and relationship is an important aspect of the way I do business. The lifetime question comes first because of its ability to focus people on their most important life goals. The second question gets them to focus on what they have to do to start accomplishing those goals.

Between these two questions is the life that connects them. You may be surprised at how many people have never taken the time to reflect on what connects their present to their vision of their future. My job is to help them make that connection, and to make sure my clients' finances support their short-term objectives while getting them to their long-term goals. The only way I can do that is by getting to know what is most important to them. That knowledge forms the basis on which all investment decisions are made; it is the rudder that keeps the investment plan on course through the up and the down and sideways moves of the markets.

Your Financial Scorecard: How a Structured Conversation Supports the Appropriate Portfolio Structure

I said at the beginning of this chapter that I believe it is important to have an in-depth, conversation with a client before even thinking about the structure of that client's portfolio. The questions mentioned previously about three-year and lifetime objectives are the starting point for that conversation. A tool I call "Your Financial Scorecard" expands and guides the conversation and ultimately helps clients frame their financial success as a foundation of success in many areas of their lives.

I'd like to show you how the major elements of Your Financial Scorecard work together to achieve this result.

The first section, Your Financial Vision, contains eight pairs of diametrically opposed statements. Clients indicate, on a scale of 5 to 1, where they stand vis-à-vis these statements. The higher their score, the clearer their financial vision. The following is what it looks like.

Your Financial Vision (excerpt)

	5	4	3	2	1	
The overall vision for my life is clear and well defined.						I don't have a clear vision of my future.
My financial goals are clear.						My financial goals are unclear.
I have a documented, step-by-step plan in place to achieve my goals.						I don't know what steps to take in order to achieve my goals.
I have a plan to connect my wealth with my important values.						My values and my wealth are not related.

These are just four of the eight pairs of statements—enough, I hope, to give you an idea of how this part of the conversation helps me assess the client's financial vision.

The second part of the Scorecard is called Your Investments and Advisors. It also contains eight pairs of statements, and clients indicate where they stand in the same way. Again, consider an example.

Your Investments and Advisors (cxcerpt)

	5	4	3	2	1	
I understand my portfolio's asset mix and it is appropriate for my needs.						I'm not sure of my portfolio's asset mix and whether it is right for me.
The fees and charges I pay are clear and understandable.						I don't know how much I pay to have my portfolio managed.
I'm very knowledgeable about investments.						I have a lot to learn about investing.
My financial advisor provides a unique level of service that meets or exceeds my expectations.						My financial advisor neither understands my needs nor provides me with an appropriate level of service.

The result of my clients' self-ratings against these statements is like a snapshot. It provides a lot of detail about what is happening right now: how they approach their lives and their investments, how organized and knowledgeable they are, whether they are getting the level of service they deserve from their current advisors, and whether they see a clear connection between their wealth and the rest of their life.

A client story may serve to illustrate how powerful this deceptively simple exercise really is. I got a call one day from an insurance specialist I often work with, asking me if I could make time to see the widow of a client of his who had died unexpectedly of a heart attack. My colleague said he had helped her sort through all the details of her husband's life insurance policy. He said the widow really needed guidance about other financial matters. I told him I'd be happy to speak to her, and she came to see me later that week.

She was a small, slight woman. Her hair was gray with a few streaks of black, and it was pulled back rather severely from a face that I can only describe as kind. Her clear blue eyes seemed even bluer in contrast to the red pantsuit that she wore, which looked expensive but was not ostentatious. Her manner was polite and very formal in that first meeting, and it has remained that way for as long as I have known her. She introduced herself simply as Mrs. Whitney, and that is what I call her to this day.

Mrs. Whitney's answers to the Scorecard questions confirmed what he had said about her.

Your Financial Vision (excerpt)

	5	4	3	2	1	
The overall vision for my life is clear and well defined.						I don't have a clear vision of my future.
My financial goals are clear.						My financial goals are unclear.
I have a documented, step-by-step plan in place to achieve my goals.						I don't know what steps to take in order to achieve my goals.
I have a plan to connect my wealth with my important values.						My values and my wealth are not related.

Your Investments and Advisors (excerpt)

	5	4	3	2	1	
I understand my portfolio's asset mix and it is appropriate for my needs.						I'm not sure of portfolio's asset mix and whether it is right for me.
The fees and charges I pay are clear and understandable.						I don't know how much I pay to have my portfolio managed.
I'm very knowl-edgeable about investments.						I have a lot to learn about investing.
My financial advisor provides a unique level of service that meets or exceeds my expectations.						My financial advisor neither understands my needs nor provides me with an appropriate level of service.

Obviously, a fairly extreme example, but not surprising for someone in her situation. In her generation it was not unusual for a husband to make all the financial decisions and take care of all the financial details, and as her responses show, Mrs. Whitney really was in the dark about how to understand and deal with her finances. Although she had had a joint chequing account with her husband, she had never even written a cheque. She did not understand her monthly bank statements, and she said her investment account statements were "like Greek to me."

• • •

She answered “NA” to the statement about values and wealth because, as she said, “I really don’t quite know what that means.” And she answered NA to the question about her financial advisor.

“Well, he was really my husband’s advisor, wasn’t he?” she said. “I never really had much to do with him. He talks to me the same way he talked to Charles, and I don’t think I understand one bit of what he says, so I’m not sure how much he understands of what I say. He just keeps telling me not to worry because he’ll look after things the way Charles would have wanted.”

She also told me her husband’s business partner was encouraging her to move all her liquid assets to the same investment counselor he used.

That was twelve years ago, and Mrs. Whitney is still my client today. Why did she decide I was the right advisor for her, and why has she stayed with me through thick and thin? I credit it to the relationship that developed as a result of our ongoing conversation and to the unparalleled level of service she enjoys with my team and me.

That day she and I discussed what she hoped to accomplish in three years and over the course of her lifetime. When I suggested she stand back a moment and try to let go of the feeling of being overwhelmed by her current situation, it turned out she actually did have a pretty clear idea of what she wanted her future to look like. Her difficulty was in seeing how the things she wanted were connected. She had indicated she did not have a clear vision of her future simply because she did not know how to put those things into a clearly articulated statement. As we talked, we were able to do this.

The simple act of clarifying and stating important long-term life and financial goals had an immediate positive effect: she felt better able to deal with the current, stress-producing realities that resulted from her husband's death. We agreed to meet the following week to discuss her situation further and what she might do to resolve her difficulties.

When we met again, we started where we had left off; that is, we continued with the structured conversation. We were both fully engaged, and I walked Mrs. Whitney through the next four steps, listing:

(1) the three greatest Dangers, Fears, or Concerns she felt she was facing at the present time.

(2) the three greatest Strengths she could use to help her achieve the goals she had articulated.

(3) the three biggest Opportunities she thought she had at the present time, *and*

(4) the three most significant Obstacles that stood in the way of her achieving her goals.

Finally, we came to the Action Steps part of the process, in which a client lists the steps to take to overcome the obstacles they identify. Mrs. Whitney's three most important Action Steps were in three different areas: financial, philanthropic, and family:

(1) Financial: Make a decision about who will manage my financial affairs—and learn enough about investments so I can understand what I've got and what's happening to it.

(2) Philanthropic: Support the Heart and Stroke Foundation both through volunteering and giving.

(3) Family: Maintain strong ties with my older son and my daughter, and strengthen my relationship with my younger son.

By articulating her goals and establishing a plan to meet them, Mrs. Whitney began the process not only of owning her financial success but also of shaping a full and rewarding future.

Chapter 4

Self-Managing Your Money:

The Three Ts of Success

It may seem ironic at first, but Mrs. Whitney's approach to owning her financial success was to entrust the management of her money to an advisor—in this case, to me. By answering the questions about short- and long-term goals and completing her Financial Scorecard, she clarified and articulated what was most important to her, and along the way she came to realize that she did not want to take the responsibility for day-to-day management of her finances. Actually, it was not so much that she came to realize that fact—after all, she first met with me because she was feeling so overwhelmed by the responsibilities that were suddenly thrust on her by her husband' death. It was more that she came to be comfortable with the fact.

Initially, she had felt she should be the one to manage her financial affairs. She said it seemed that every time she turned on the television she saw ads for investment companies that let you do your own buying and selling, and they always featured ordinary-looking people who seemed to be successful at it. Besides, her husband had made the money, and he had left it to her, and she felt this must have been a vote of confidence on his part that she could manage it. In fact, though, it may simply have been a failure on his part to do adequate estate planning, because Mrs. Whitney clearly did not have the combination of characteristics that make for successful self-management of investments.

I call these characteristics the Three Ts of successful investing: Time, Temperament, and Talent. The time to devote to the daily, weekly, monthly, and annual routines required by sound financial management. The temperament to withstand the strong emotional pull of greed and fear, to assess market behavior objectively, to act only when there are rational reasons for doing so—in other words, the temperament to stick to your game plan. And the talent to gain knowledge and understanding of how the economy and the capital markets work, to grasp the sometimes complex interrelationships of market forces.

One problem I often encounter, though, is that many people are like Mrs. Whitney: they feel they should be able to do it all by themselves. It's a funny thing: people do not feel they are remiss for not taking care of their own dental health; they do not feel a sense of personal inadequacy in letting a trained dentist do it for them, or in seeking an experienced orthodontist to put braces on their children's teeth. When it comes to investments, however, many think managing money should be like any other do-it-yourself task. But it is not.

Some people have two of the three Ts, some have one, and some have none; it is the rare person who has the time, the temperament, and the talent to look after their investments adequately. In my quarter century of experience in the investment business, I have seen only a rare few achieve any real, consistent success in managing their own financial affairs.

A few client stories will illustrate time, temperament, and talent in a more tangible, personal way. Let's start with someone who had everything but time.

Time

Tempus fugit.
–Virgil (70 BCE-19 BCE)

Everyone knows this familiar adage: Time flies. And these days, it seems, time flies faster and more furiously than ever. It is probably no coincidence that cinematic technique has shifted over the last generation or so. Movies used to be made up of a series of relatively long, slow scenes; now the pace is more akin to a kaleidoscopic montage, with modern-day movies made up of much shorter and faster-paced scenes. Is this life imitating art or art reflecting the reality of life? It is hard to say.

What is certain, though, is that many people today lead busy, full, fast-paced lives with what may seem like a thousand different demands on their time and attention. Work is demanding. Raising children is demanding. Maintaining strong relationships is demanding. All of these things are important; all of them take time; and we owe it to ourselves, to our families, and to our employers, to give them all the time they deserve.

Let me tell you about John L. I first met John relatively early in my career, when I was still working on the institutional desk at Merrill Lynch. He was a successful portfolio manager for a large pension fund. This fund was one of my clients, and John was one of the portfolio managers I dealt with there. He was noted for being studious, and his looks fit his reputation. He was in his mid-forties,and he looked out at the world through the kind of wire-rimmed glasses his grandfather might have worn.

Over the years we came to develop respect for each other. I became convinced that he completely deserved his reputation as a financial wizard. I often thought back then that he must be wildly successful in his own investing; after all, he was recognized time and again as being among the top three percent of portfolio managers in Canada. If anyone was qualified to manage money, it was John.

For his part, he told me he appreciated the fact that I never wasted his time when I came to him with an equity idea because I knew the characteristics of the types of stocks he was interested in, I always did my homework, and I presented solid ideas that fell within the parameters of his investment mandate.

It is telling that John focused on time when he told me this, because it was precisely the fact he had so little time that led him to become my client when I left the institutional side of the business. Let me explain.

I ran into John by chance shortly after had I moved to the private client side. We chatted and I told him about the change in direction I had chosen for my career. John congratulated me and said he'd love to talk more about it, but (you can probably guess what comes next) he didn't have the time right then. We agreed to meet over lunch the following week.

When we did get together, John told me he had been looking for someone he could trust to manage his personal investments. He laughed when he said it was a perfect example of the shoemaker's children having no shoes—he was spending so much time working on behalf of his clients, managing millions upon millions of dollars in investments, that he never seemed to have the time or energy left over to focus on his own financial health. Because of our past professional relationship, he wished to entrust that responsibility to me.

I managed his investments for years, and when he was planning his retirement, I advised him about how best to restructure his affairs for this new and exciting chapter in his life. I expected he would want to manage his investments himself now that time was not such an issue.

John certainly had the temperament and the talent for managing money. However, like so many of my clients who have professional careers, initially he was time-starved and unable to manage his own money. When he reached retirement, and now had all the time he needed, he decided to spend it doing other things. I was pleasantly surprised and thoroughly delighted when he told me he wanted me to continue as his advisor.

Now let's visit someone who had more than enough time but definitely not the right temperament.

Temperament

No passion so effectually robs the mind of its powers of acting and reasoning as fear.
–Edmund Burke (1729-1797)

Why do I start this section with a quotation about fear? Because fear is one of the two emotions that consistently cause people to stray from the investment plans they have worked out for themselves. Although Burke lived more than two hundred years ago, he might as well have been writing about the influence of fear on the modern investor. In fact, I can't think of anyone who has expressed that influence so well, because it is precisely in the area of investing that we can best see how fear weakens minds.

Many investors, even those who have taken the time to put together a short- and long-term plan, are paralyzed by fear when markets take an unexpected and substantial fall—and believe me, even if market pundits have been calling for months for the market to retrench, do-it-yourself investors almost always find the retrenchment a surprise. To them it may seem the world is coming to an end. Like a deer caught in the headlights, many seem unable to act.

Likewise, many seem to lose the power of rational thought. They lose sight of their goals altogether; they seem to forget that their short-term objectives are the steps that will help them achieve their long-term objectives. Those who can act often take their money out of the market at or near the bottom, with no clear plan for when they will get back in.

Greed is another emotion that holds great sway over investors. The promise of easy money wreaks havoc with investment portfolios, motivating people to abandon their plans, act on tips, and hold on to stocks they have fallen in love with because they just know "this one's going to make it." Meanwhile, their carefully planned strategies, the balance of risk and reward they had so diligently built into their portfolio—all this flies out the window.

I hope none of this sounds too familiar to you, but if it does you might ask yourself whether you have the right temperament for managing investments. Gerald S. certainly did not.

Gerald had built and operated a successful business for more than thirty years. Although he always thought he would keep the business in the family, he received an unsolicited bid for it one day. Suffice it to say, it was an offer he could not refuse: he could sell most of the company and keep one operating division for his son to run. Suddenly he went from being a hard-working entrepreneur with a comfortable lifestyle to a very wealthy man who no longer needed to work.

Gerald's wife had been a client of mine for some time. She had inherited a substantial sum of money before Gerald had sold his company, and as a result of our structured conversation and her Scorecard answers, we had determined together that her portfolio should be fairly conservative but with some exposure to growth. She was comfortable with the balance of risk and reward, and she was satisfied with her portfolio's returns over the years.

Gerald was not a client of mine at the time. Before the buyout, he had been a "player" when it came to investments; that is, he was always chasing the hot stock, looking for the hot tips that would pay off really big. Most of his money was tied up in the business, so he did not have a lot of money in the markets. He had some successes, as this type of investor sometimes does; he had even more disappointments. Luckily, most of his money was tied up in the business and therefore not in the markets, so his "investing" did not affect his net worth in any substantial way.

When the sale went through, he chose to place his investments in the hands of an advisor who was a friend of his son. Although they started out with a well-structured portfolio, Gerald kept playing the market, actively trading low-priced stocks in mining, pharmaceuticals, technology—you name it. Before long, the portfolio bore no resemblance to its original structure. The real trouble, though, was that Gerald was now using, and losing, substantial amounts of money. Even though the sale had given him what most would consider to be quite a fortune, the promise of the big payoff and the anticipation of the thrill of winning kept motivating him to trade, trade, trade. His net worth was beginning to suffer.

One day out of the blue, I got a call from Gerald. He was in a panic. He had just lost a significant amount of money on one of his bets.

"Susan, you've been doing a pretty good job for Elizabeth, and now I want to see what you can do for me," he said. "I'm transferring my account to you."

And then he said, "As soon as the paperwork clears, I want you to buy fifteen hundred shares of XYZ Corporation. There's big news coming out, and the stock's going to go through the roof!"

I told Gerald I appreciated his confidence in me and then I explained a bit about the way I conduct my business. I invited him to come in and talk to me before he decided to make a change.

The long and the short of it is that Gerald did move his account over to me—most of it, that is. I explained my investment philosophy to him, how his investments would be structured, and why they would be structured that way. I also explained we would not deviate from the plan on a whim. He liked what he heard. He knew he needed someone to provide the discipline he could not muster himself. In the end, though, he decided to leave some money—I call it his sandbox money—with his other advisor. It was a perfect solution for someone who needed the thrill of do-it-yourself investing: he could still play around, do trades, and chase the big pay-off with his sandbox money, but the amount was finite and contained, so he could not really do himself much damage. And he got serious about his serious money.

Talent

We are always more anxious to be distinguished for a talent which we do not possess, than to be praised for the fifteen we do possess.
–Mark Twain (1835-1910)

What are your fifteen talents? Perhaps investment management is among them, perhaps not. But if you've ever been to a cocktail party, you know there are many people who want to be thought of as extremely talented in this area. They do not want you to think they were just lucky when they bought low and sold high; they do not want you to think it was by chance that they identified the takeover target a month before its price jumped on the news, or that they went into cash just days before the market collapsed. No, they want you to realize how smart, how talented they are. There's a certain cachet, a certain kind of status, that investment success bestows on an individual. Unfortunately, many of those who aspire to this talent simply do not have it.

That is in no way a slight. It can be said of any talent you can name. Think of any demonstration of talent you have witnessed lately. Maybe you were lucky enough to be at the Vancouver Olympics to see the skiers or the curlers or the skaters or any of the other athletes who showcased their talent there.

You may have remarked to a friend that it all seemed so effortless, so natural. You know, of course, that it was not effortless. You know about the years and years of training that Olympic athletes endure for their one shot at the podium. You know how hard all these performers had to work to master their craft and make their performance seem so effortless, and you undoubtedly realize that no amount of work could have produced the results you witnessed if the people had not had talent in the first place. In his book Outliers, author Malcolm Gladwell goes so far as to suggest it takes ten thousand hours of practice at something to achieve real expertise!

I think Mrs. Whitney's story illustrates how important talent is if you are going to manage your own money. It is simply a fact: some people have a talent for investment management; some do not. Mrs. Whitney, through no fault of her own, did not. On one level, the talent for investment management is a knack for reading situations and events in a certain way, an ability to see connections between things that others just do not see. Those who have this talent, and who develop it through hard work, by acquiring knowledge about the economy and market dynamics, by learning about the many different types of investment securities, by learning how to analyze a company's operations, and by years of experience—they are the ones who become successful money managers. They make it look easy, but we know it is not.

Chapter 5

Business Owners:

Special Needs, Unique Solutions

Happily, my clients come from all walks of life, which means my team and I have the pleasure of meeting and getting to know all sorts of people. We enjoy the challenges and the constant stimulation that come as a result of dealing with people who make their livings in so many different ways. My investment philosophy shapes the relationships I have with all of my clients equally, no matter what the source of their wealth may be, and ensures that each gets precisely the services they need and want.

Some of my clients are business owners who have built successful family businesses in many different industries, including the service industry, manufacturing, and distribution—with operations ranging from shoes to plastics, from mining to technology, from baby clothes to communications and marketing. To a point, these clients are alike and I get to know them in the same way: they answer the same questions about three-year and lifetime goals, they complete their Financial Scorecard, and they articulate their short- and long-term goals. Only when this process is complete do I propose an appropriate investment plan for them.

I say to a point because there is a point at which they begin to differ in significant ways: the point at which they begin to plan how they will transition out of their business. Suddenly, their need for advice becomes much more complex. I have spoken about how my practice is based on an intensive service model, and in this chapter I would like to describe a multifaceted service tailored specifically to the needs of business owners who find themselves at this stage in the life of their company.

Business people become successful because of their ability to recognize opportunity and their knack for taking the right risks at the right time.

However, while they are able to plan and execute a successful growth strategy for their company, many business owners do not know how to plan and execute a successful transition strategy.

As business owners discover when they think about stepping back from their business, the transitioning of a business is not an event; it is a process. It almost always involves the owner's desire to realize some or all of the value of their company. In most cases, therefore, the process triggers a transaction through which the business owner extracts value from the business. There are several ways to do this. The owner can refinance the business, or sell the business over time to the next generation of the family, or sell the business outright, or find an equity partner to assist in the transition. Although successful business owners build significant wealth as they build their businesses, the bulk of their wealth is often tied up in the business. For many, therefore, regardless of which option they choose, the transaction results in an exponential leap in their liquid wealth.

This is especially true for owners who decide to sell their business outright to a third party, because they realize the full value of their business immediately; those who keep the business in the family normally realize only a portion of the value in cash.

So, you may be wondering exactly how my service model can help in this process. Fortunately, my service model includes access to a network of professionals who are experts in the many areas a business owner must consider when deciding about a transition.

An Informal Network of Formidable Expertise

Most business owners are neither trained nor prepared for the transition of their business. In addition, their professional advisors are often straight jacketed into a particular area of expertise or may not feel comfortable challenging their client's thinking. But when deciding how to transition their business, business owners require the specialized advice of professionals who have both the experience and the courage to go beyond the traditional approach.

Business owners naturally want the best possible outcome from the planning they do, and the best possible outcome means many things. It means deciding whether to keep the business in the family or to sell all or part of it to a third party. It means deciding who will run the business if they do keep it in the family—a family member or a professional manager who is not family.

If a business owner decides to sell all or part of the business, the best possible outcome means more than getting the best price for it. It means structuring the sale in the most tax-efficient manner to retain as much of the sale price as possible. It means investing the proceeds, a responsibility that many business owners find daunting and one that may include using insurance in innovative ways as well. And it means considering the impact of the sale on their family.

The fact is, transition planning is almost always closely tied to another reality: retirement. People often look ahead to retirement with a sense of excitement and adventure, but retirement almost inevitably engenders other feelings as well. Business owners sometimes wonder what not being in business will do to their sense of identity, and retiring people in general are at a stage when they think about their mortality—they start looking at their lives not from the point of view of how many years are behind them but how many years are ahead. They wonder whether their investments are structured properly for a long and comfortable retirement.

You may be surprised that I include families when I talk about the best possible outcome of transitioning a business, but whatever the final decision—to keep the business or to sell it—the best possible outcome also means figuring out what is best for those you love. Resolving the sometimes thorny interpersonal issues that can arise among members of a business family is an essential element of a sound plan. And it is almost never easy to do.

Planning for a business transition often reminds business owners to revisit their estate plan, or to establish an estate plan if they do not have one already. In fact, many have overlooked this important responsibility altogether, and others have given it only cursory thought.

As you can see, planning successfully for the transition of a family-owned business is a complex process that necessarily involves many areas of expertise: corporate finance, tax planning, estate planning, investment planning, insurance planning, and dealing with family dynamics, to name a few. As a result of watching some of my business-owner clients struggle through the transition process, I have forged relationships with a number of independent professionals who specialize in these many areas, and together we constitute an informal network that can guide and support a business owner through the transition. We have found it is most effective to work collaboratively, first to ensure that business owners achieve clarity about what they want and then to structure their deal in a way that delivers exactly that.

Because of the degree of collaboration we have developed, each of us understands the type of information the others need. This allows us to share pertinent information with one another, which saves the business owner time and energy by not having to answer the same questions innumerable times. This also provides the opportunity to identify interdependencies and discuss various options among ourselves, which helps us come up with a seamless, coordinated strategy that meets the business owner's objectives for all aspects of the transition. The end result of collaboration is to ensure the most effective solutions based on the clients' situation.

• • •

Coordinating the activities of many different advisory professionals may seem daunting. And in fact it can be. That is why it works best for the business owner when one of these advisors functions also as a kind of quarterback. When this happens, the business owner has a person to organize the work of the others and the flow of information from the business owner to the advisors and among the advisors themselves. This helps ensure that the business owner can continue to focus on the business and not be distracted by myriad demands on their time and attention from many different people.

Not all business owners need the services of everyone in this network. They use their own trusted advisors when they are qualified to advise on such a major transaction, and they work with those of my colleagues who can provide the kind of advice their own advisors lack the requisite expertise and experience to deliver. When business owners do retain some of their own advisors, we welcome the opportunity to work with them as part of a collaborative team. The business owner chooses which of us to work with, and we become involved in the process at different times, as needed.

Some have told us they think our approach represents a best-in-class, just-in-time model for transition planning, one that serves their interests better than the one-stop shopping model employed by some companies that advise on business transitions.

Another piece of advice for business owners is it is never too early to start planning.

Starting the transition plan early has many advantages including: ability to get the most value for the business, understanding the best time to sell, tax minimization, and reduced stress on the business owner and the family. Another benefit is that early planning allows your advisors time to formulate a strategic investment plan putting the proceeds of the sale to work immediately rather than waiting on the sidelines.

Edward M. Gets Ready to Sell

I make sure my clients who are business owners know about this network of experts, and that they have a good understanding of the complexity of the transition process. When they need advice about transitioning out of their business, they often ask me to arrange introductions to the professionals in my network.

Edward M. is an example of just such a client. He had built a very successful chain of medical supply stores. People thought it was funny that his company was associated with medicine. He was medium height, medium weight, had brown hair and brown eyes and an unassuming presence—he came across more like a friendly family doctor than a successful businessman.

Edward had not actually been thinking of selling his business. In fact, he hoped it would be a family business for generations and was grooming one of his sons to take over. Not that he was thinking of retiring any time soon. He was still relatively young and expected to be working for at least another ten or twelve years.

Edward had met someone at a conference in Chicago in 1995 who ran the same type of business as his in the U.S. Midwest and Northeast. They hit it off right away, compared notes about their companies, stayed in touch after the conference, and over the years became friends. Several times this man had broached the subject of buying Edward's company, but Edward had never encouraged him to take the conversation any further. Then one day his friend called with an actual offer, one that was generous enough to make Edward consider it seriously.

He phoned me and explained what had happened and said he wanted to meet with a couple of people in my network, specifically the corporate finance and the tax advisors. Although the offer seemed like a tremendous amount of money, he was not sure whether it reflected fair market value for his company. And if he was going to entertain the offer, he was also going to negotiate some of its terms, so he wanted advice on how to structure the deal in the most tax-effective way.

With the help of the corporate finance specialist, he determined that he could probably get a bit more for his company than what was initially offered. In addition, the tax advisor recommended a deal structure that would result in a very low double-digit taxation of the proceeds of sale if the deal went through. Long story short, Edward negotiated a deal that resulted in the proverbial "offer I couldn't refuse." He ended up selling his company for $21.6 million, 8% above the buyer's first offer of $20 million.

After the Transaction

It is, of course, after the transaction that the investment plan is executed, because it is only then that the funds are available for investment. The optimal scenario, though, is for me to become involved before the transaction date so I can develop an investment plan that is ready for execution as soon as the funds are received in the account. This is what happened in Edward's case.

Not that there wasn't competition for the money. In a deal of this size, word gets out.

Everyone was after Edward to manage his money. He was straightforward with me about this. He told me he would be meeting with other advisors to see what they recommended, and I told him I would do the same if I were in his shoes.

Edward had a close relationship with his bank manager, as every business owner would. The manager wanted to introduce him to the people from the bank's investment arm, and Edward agreed to meet with them. Edward told me that when the meeting took place, he felt they really didn't really take the time to understand all the aspects his situation and that the solutions they had to offer were cookie cutter. He was also surprised that they did not seem interested in meeting with Edward's other advisors; they simply wanted to deal with the proceeds of the sale.

It is not surprising that this approach did not work for Edward. He was the typical hands-on entrepreneur. He was used to being in control of his world, deciding what would happen and when it would happen and how it would happen.

He also met with advisors from two other firms but felt neither had the depth of experience he was looking for; the plans they proposed confirmed this feeling, he said.

In the end, Edward decided the plan I had proposed was right for him. It was, in fact, the only proposal that satisfied his rather unusual set of requirements. He was concerned about cash flow. He considered his company to be "the goose that laid the golden egg"; it had always provided a steady income stream. Now that it was gone, he wanted to make sure he would have a comfortable level of income from his investments. He wanted income of $1 million a year, and he wanted to leave an estate of $20 million to his two sons.

A tall order, yes. And one I would not have been able to deliver on if not for the network of specialists I described above. Any financial advisor should be able to take a portfolio of $21.6 million and generate $1 million of annual income. But how do you do that and still preserve $20 million for the estate? I met with the insurance specialist in my network and went over Edward's requirements, and he came up with an innovative insurance solution that would help deliver an estate of that amount, even with Edward taking income of $1 million every year.
Edward also met with an estate lawyer who is part of my network, and she devised an estate plan to ensure that his wishes for his wife and his two sons would be fulfilled.

In the end, it was really understanding more than just the money part that solidified my relationship with Edward. I understood that he and his wife were excited about this sudden windfall; I understood, too, that they were somewhat unsettled by it. He had been a hard-working businessman, and she had resumed her career in social work once the younger boy started university. They had always been comfortable but they had lived a relatively modest lifestyle. Now they were wealthy and he no longer had his work. What would he do? And would she continue to work or retire along with him? Where did they fit in now? What shape would their life take going forward?

I do not claim to have answered all of these questions for them. I will say, though, and I know they would agree, that helping them frame the questions helped them establish new directions in their lives.

Chapter 6

Women and Money:

You've Come a Long Way, Baby
… or Have You?

You may recognize the slogan from the Virginia Slims cigarette ads, which first appeared in July 1968. The marketers were clearly hoping to cash in on the changing place of women in modern society, and their advertising worked. Women had indeed come a long way in so many realms.

A recent TIME magazine Special Report on Women is filled with statistics illustrating just how much a woman's world has continued to change since that first ad. Some examples:

Between 1972 and 2008, the percentage of jobs held by women increased from 36.2 to 49.8, and the percentage of women college students increased from 43 to 57. From 1970 to 2008, the percentage of women lawyers jumped from 3 to 32, and the percentage of women doctors from 8 to 28.

These are impressive gains, but what about another important area: women's ability to understand their money? In my practice I have seen women who are extremely knowledgeable about investments and women who have never even written a cheque. I have seen women at all stages and in all phases of life, and each stage and phase seems to have its own set of challenges. This chapter is not intended as an investment primer for women. Rather, it includes some of my observations about three categories of single women I have worked with—widows, women who are divorced or in the process of divorce, and women who have never married—to highlight some of the difficult issues these women face when it comes to managing their wealth. Then I'll share the secret that brings them peace of mind.

The Widow's Walk

In seaside towns on the East Coast and elsewhere, you will see grand houses with a railed platform on the roof. The platform often has a cupola at the centre, usually glassed in on all four sides and usually fairly small. The platform is referred to as a widow's walk. It is said that sailor's wives would walk there when their husband's ships were due in harbour, watching for that first glimpse of white sail to tell them everything was all right; in foul weather the wives would watch from the cupola. It was called the widow's walk because all too often the ships never appeared.

Whether it is a reliable story or not, it is certainly true that many widows today seem lost when it comes to dealing with family wealth—wealth that becomes their responsibility quite suddenly the day they become widows.

You've already met Mrs. Whitney, and her story exemplifies the plight of wealthy women of a certain age, women who have limited experience handling money. Partly as a result of the social norms of their time (the man being breadwinner, the woman being homemaker), many of these women simply did not have to think about money; the man was the provider and he always provided well. Unfortunately, we find all too often that the husband neglected one all-important aspect of wealth management, that is, establishing a sound estate plan—figuring out in the present the best way to provide for his loved ones once he was gone.

I do not want to give the impression that women cannot become quite savvy about financial affairs. I could not write this book if that were the case; I would be in a very different kind of career.

Some women of Mrs. Whitney's era, of course, wanted a much more active involvement in family finances, and they learned how to do a budget and how to run a household on that budget. In my experience, women often demonstrate remarkable attention to detail and are usually willing to admit they don't know something and to seek help in finding out what they want to know. It is not surprising, then, that some also learned a great deal about investing. The ones I want to focus on here, though, more often fit into the limited-knowledge category, and they have certain characteristics in common with Mrs. Whitney.

First of all, they feel bewildered. Added to the grief of losing a husband is the burden of having to make decisions about how their money will be managed and who will manage it. They usually have family advisors who recommend a course of action, but most often they were the husband's advisors; these women, with their limited investment knowledge, often worry about whether the advice they are getting is right for them. No wonder they feel overwhelmed.

Some widows have no idea how much money they need in order to continue living as they have been living. They do not know their weekly or monthly or annual expenses. As a result, they often worry about whether their husbands have left enough for them to live on. Others seem unconcerned about this; they live as though there will always be enough … but often this question lurks beneath the surface. It is a fairly common concern.

Many women are actively involved in charitable work of one kind or another, volunteering their time or their money or both to causes they believe in. When they become widows, their charitable and philanthropic instincts do not suddenly stop. They often worry, however, about how much they can afford to donate and whether there will be enough at the end of their lives to bequeath to their favourite charities.

What can these (mostly) older women possibly have in common with a divorced woman in middle age? The one-word answer is: uncertainty.

• • •

Divorcing ... Divorcing ... Divorced

From the moment of decision about divorce to the moment the divorce settlement agreement is signed, sealed, and delivered, a woman's life can be filled with uncertainties of many kinds. In the midst of often wrenching emotional conflicts there are many practical matters for her to consider. If there are children still living at home, what will the custody arrangements be? What about child support? University tuition? What will happen to the marital home? And to the family cottage? Will she be facing a decline in her standard of living?

For women who have never worked outside the home, the prospect of seeking and finding decent employment can be daunting. So, these women may think to themselves, "Okay, so maybe we've come a long way, but look where I am right now!"

Even women doctors, lawyers, and other professionals, who make a very comfortable living, worry about the economic impact of divorce on themselves and their children. These women have worked hard to establish themselves in their careers; they are proud of their personal achievements and proud that through them they have been able to contribute to the opportunities their children enjoy. Whether these include private schools, travel, summer camps, or summer courses in Europe, the prospect of divorce suddenly puts question marks where previously there were only happy exclamation points.

The Bag-Lady Syndrome

You would be surprised at the number of single female professionals—women who own their own homes and have accumulated significant savings—who nonetheless worry they will end up penniless.

Let me give you an example. A woman lawyer named Sarah C., in her mid-forties and never married, was referred to me by one of my clients. He said Sarah had been extremely successful in her career but was unhappy with her current advisor, although he did not say why. He simply said she had told him she wanted to interview others to see if she could find a better fit.

When Sarah came to my office, the first thing I thought was that she was the very definition of good taste. Dressed in a gray Chanel suit with a gray silk blouse and wearing a double string of black pearls, she looked elegant and completely self-possessed. As we talked, I realized she was quite comfortable talking about the investment process; she obviously knew a lot about the subject.

As I do with everyone who comes to see me, I explained the structured conversation I have with new people and why I have it. Sarah said it sounded like a good approach, and so we started. She became more and more relaxed as the conversation continued, although she maintained her professional poise. That is, she maintained it right up to the point when I asked her to talk about any fears she might have about not being able to meet her long-term objectives.

Suddenly she looked a little tentative, as if she were deciding whether to tell me something or not.

"Susan, you may think I'm crazy," she said after a short pause, "but I'm a huge Lily Tomlin fan, and my biggest fear is that I'm going to end up just like her character Trudy, the crazy bag lady. I mean, there's only me—I've been single all my life, and it doesn't look like that's going to change. There are certainly no kids in the picture to help me in my old age. My future depends on me. And I keep being afraid my life will be like Trudy's when I'm seventy-five, collecting bottles and hanging them on my grocery cart as I push it aimlessly along."

Believe me, she is not alone. I have heard this story innumerable times from single women who have very much in common with Sarah: high income, substantial accumulated assets, and a gnawing sense of uncertainty about the future.

There is that word again: uncertainty. What can be done about it?

How Much Is Enough?

It is indeed uncertainty that links these women in my mind. They are of different ages, they are in different stages of their lives, and they find themselves in very different circumstances, but they are all facing one big, basic question: "How much is enough?" This is the question at the root of all their worries, because if you do not know how much is enough, then you are always going to worry about how much you have.

The good news is that there is an answer that fits everyone who asks this question. And the answer starts with another question: "How much is enough for what?" In other words, you can never figure out how much money is enough until you figure out what you want that money to do. Once you know what you want the money to do, deciding the amount you need comes down to a fairly straightforward set of calculations and projections.

You have already read how I worked with Mrs. Whitney to help her articulate her wishes for how she wanted to live and what she wanted to accomplish during the rest of her life. By educating her about how to make sense of her financial statements, my team and I helped her achieve a feeling of control whereas before she had felt only bewilderment. When all the estate assets were accounted for, we sat down with her and explained her financial situation to her. And once she had prioritized her long-term goals, we provided sound, reasonable, conservative projections that eased her worries about whether she would have enough to accomplish her goals. We do the same not just for elderly widows, but also for all of our clients.

Let me tell you how this played out in the case of a woman who was in the middle of a very messy divorce. Diane S. was a strikingly beautiful woman in her late thirties, a natural blonde with cobalt-blue eyes and refined, classical features—when I first met her I was actually startled by her resemblance to Grace Kelly in Alfred Hitchcock's Rear Window.

Diane was determined, as she put it, to "get every cent from him I can." The divorce had come as a surprise to her, there was another woman involved, and Diane felt betrayed and angry.

I asked her to try to put those feelings aside for a moment, to look at her new reality as objectively as possible, and to think realistically about what her new goals would be over the next three years and over her lifetime. It was a revealing conversation. It helped her focus on what she wanted for her children. I asked her to think about whether she really wanted everything she could possibly get from her husband, which could involve years of expensive and emotionally draining court battles … or enough to achieve the goals she had just articulated. She opted for the latter, we worked out how much she would need, and she reached an attractive, reasonable settlement with a minimum of strain.

We did the same thing for Sarah C. Starting with her goals, her current assets, and her income and expenses (both current expenses and anticipated expenses in retirement), we did projections for her until the age of one hundred. Guess what? She could finally see that no two people on earth could be more different than she and Trudy the bag lady!

Chapter 7

Inheritance:

Wind in Your Sails …
or Albatross Around Your Neck?

For those who have no prospect of inheriting significant wealth, the idea of doing so often seems like the very thing that would finally put the wind in their sails for good. It is just a happy fantasy. Many ideas vie for first place in an exhilarating rush of thinking that goes something like this: No more mortgage! Whoosh. Any car I want! Whoosh. First-class vacations … any time I want! Whoosh. First-class everything! No more work! Freedom at last! Whoosh and whoosh and whoosh—money the pleasant breeze that never dies down.

The reality for those who actually do inherit wealth, though, could hardly be more different; too often their inheritance can feel like an albatross around their neck.

That may sound counterintuitive, so let me explain what I mean.

Many successful people have the experience of working hard to get ahead and establish a comfortable lifestyle. They have generated adequate savings to ensure that they can maintain that same degree of comfort throughout their lives, whether they live to be one hundred years old. They rightly feel a certain pride of accomplishment. They are proud not just of what they have been able to acquire, but perhaps even more importantly, of the very thing that made their success possible in the first place: the competence and expertise they have developed in their chosen field.

Most of us do not have the experience of inheriting money that we didn't make. But when we stop to think about it, we realize that this is exactly what an inheritance is: it is money that someone else made and now is entrusting to others. The fact that someone else made the money means it often comes with strings attached—strings and a lot of strong feelings.

The strings can come in the form of trusts or foundations established by the benefactor with restrictions on how the wealth is to be invested and how and when it can be accessed.

The feelings are sometimes positive, like a feeling of responsibility for looking after the inheritance, preserving it, even enhancing it so it can be passed on to the next generation. Sometimes inheriting wealth can engender negative feelings, too: feelings of not deserving the money because someone else made it, feelings of guilt that no matter how hard or how long most people work they will probably never attain the degree of wealth that has simply been given to them. As we will soon see, strong positive and strong negative feelings can both play out in good and bad ways.

Give Until It Hurts?

The experience of one of my clients illustrates how this kind of guilt about an inheritance can motivate a person's actions.

Sonia G. came from a wealthy family and inherited a large sum of money at a relatively young age. She never felt entirely comfortable with having so much money, and because she was extremely generous by nature she decided philanthropic pursuits made a lot of sense for her. She established an organization to support literacy and poured money into it. It gave her great satisfaction to know her money was making a tangible difference in people's lives, and also knowing that their improved literacy would mean more opportunities for them down the road. Something good came from Sonia's discomfort about her inheritance.

At the same time, though, Sonia also developed a reputation as a soft touch. People would approach her with such lines as, "We can't get a mortgage at the bank. Will you give us a mortgage so we can buy a house?" Or, "My husband needs to go to the United States for special chemotherapy treatment that's not available here, but we can't afford it. Can you help us out?" The requests were endless, and Sonia's response was always yes. Something bad came from Sonia's guilt about her money: a feeling that she had so much and that these other people were asking for what seemed so little in comparison.

When Sonia came to talk to me about handling her investments, she mentioned these "endless little requests" for money with a dismissive smile, as if they were really nothing.

"I just can't bring myself to say no to these things," she said. "And besides, giving to these requests isn't really hurting me, is it?"

Sonia agreed to let me contact her accountant to determine how much money she had given to such requests over the past three years. When I received his report I saw the amount was not little at all. In fact, I have seen small foundations that distributed less in annual grants! We factored this unofficial charitable giving into the projections we were putting together for Sonia. When she came back to see me to go over the investment plan I was proposing, she was shocked to see exactly how much she had been giving away and how seriously it was eroding her capital. There was a very real danger she would exhaust her assets before old age.

A sobering experience for Sonia, to say the least. She said seeing it all worked out on paper made it seem real: she could see in black and white that the rate at which she was randomly distributing assets was unsustainable.

The solution? Strategic philanthropy: we helped Sonia determine the most significant causes she wanted to support, we did the research to determine where her money would do the most good, we figured out how much she could reasonably contribute each year, and we now oversee her charitable giving as part of her overall wealth management plan.

The result? Sonia will not run out of money in her lifetime. In addition, although she may still feel a bit guilty about it, she can now say no to inappropriate requests for money—and blame it on us!

Responsible Stewardship I: *Preserve That Capital!*

I mentioned above the many feelings associated with receiving an inheritance. A feeling of responsibility for prudent stewardship is often one of them. Whether that feeling produces beneficial or harmful results depends entirely on how "responsible stewardship" is defined.

For some heirs, being responsible means working to preserve and enhance the value of the inheritance, to the point that this becomes their sole focus. The desire not to squander the inheritance is certainly commendable, but the inherited wealth often becomes the defining fact of family life, and managing that wealth becomes the family business.

Establishment and management of trusts and family holding companies, discovery and utilization of tax-saving strategies, overseeing investments or investment managers—these all become part of the life's work of family members. This can be all to the good if this is the kind of work the family members want to pursue. Too often, though, the very structures put in place to preserve the wealth, the processes established for its management, and the strictures placed on how the wealth can be used can co-opt any real personal choice in the matter. Why? Because the structures and the strictures and the investment processes have all been designed around a kind of one-dimensional objective: preserve the money and make it grow.

• • •

From a certain point of view this makes perfect sense. It is often the point of view of the generation who are direct inheritors, and it often involves emotional as well as rational considerations. The thinking goes something like this: "Dad spent his whole life creating this wealth, and now he's leaving it to us. We have a responsibility to him to see that it is invested wisely so we can pass it on to our heirs."

This line of reasoning seems sound and logical. But do you see a problem with it? I do. Because of the emphasis on the wealth itself, it implies that the responsibility to the benefactor to preserve the wealth overrides all responsibilities to the next generation except that of preserving the wealth. And the expectation is that the next generation will then preserve the wealth for their heirs. But what happens to individuals who may want to do something different with their lives than carry out a prescribed role in the wealth-preservation plan?

In this definition of responsible stewardship, the wealth-management machinery can trump an individual's ambition if that individual's ambition is not directed toward the family wealth-management enterprise. This is an ironic turn of events, because in all likelihood the wealth was created in the first place by someone who developed competence and expertise by following their own ambition. For the heir who hears the beat of a different drum, the family wealth can feel like an albatross around their neck, impeding them from developing their abilities in areas that are personally meaningful.

The issue of foundations set up by a benefactor can complicate the management of family money even further. When there is a great deal of money, setting up a foundation can make a lot of sense. But what happens when there are many beneficiaries, all with different interests and different directions in their lives, who feel forcibly confined by the investment mandate of the foundation? What happens generations later when presumably the family has continued to grow and the interests and pursuits are even more divergent? It is no wonder that families almost always look to professional advisors to manage foundation money. They need someone who is experienced with this type of investing in order to ensure that the interests of all beneficiaries are taken into account.

I fully appreciate the desire of wealthy families to maintain their wealth; after all, that is my core business: preservation and growth of capital. However, I have worked with wealthy families who define responsible stewardship differently and who have therefore put different types of structures in place to accomplish their goal of shepherding their wealth. They have done it in a way that respects and supports individual initiative on the part of family members.

Responsible Stewardship II: ***What Is the Money For?***

Let me tell you about a family that has managed successfully to maintain and enhance their wealth through several generations in a way that provides family members with the opportunity to pursue personal goals that are not directly connected to the enterprise of managing the family wealth.

Instead of starting with the question, "How can we make this money grow?" they asked, "What is this money for?" They reasoned that certainly some of the money was for their own support. So they figured out how much money they needed in order to continue to live well, to cover their ongoing living expenses and whatever indulgences and luxuries they might want. Erring on the side of generous, they earmarked a certain amount of money for "family maintenance," and invested it so the income covered their needs.

There was still a great deal of money left, and they asked themselves the same question again, but with a slightly different emphasis: "What is this money for?" You will probably not be surprised to hear that there were lots of opinions in response to this question. As it turns out, one of the things they all agreed on was that they should give some of the money away. They had already figured out how much was enough for them, and they reasoned that there were many worthy causes that could benefit from their financial support. So, after lengthy and often passionate discussion, they came to agreement about certain causes they wanted to support, and they gave some of their "excess" money to a number of charitable organizations.

"I never really felt the power of my wealth until I realized how much good it could do for others," one family member told me.

Even after this there was still a substantial amount of money left, and it was invested along with the family maintenance money. The family is now several generations removed from the original creator of the wealth, and there are many branches of the family, with numerous cousins in various parts of the country. Because of the wealth-management structures they put in place, the family money is well cared for, but it serves the family members rather than mastering them.

When the management of family wealth is approached with careful thought given not only to the protection and growth of capital but also to the growth and nurturing of family members, then wealth is neither a carefree breeze nor an albatross. It is not a breeze because in fact it does demand mature and responsible stewardship, which means ensuring that it is invested prudently and being vigilant about its management. And it is not an albatross because it becomes a powerful enabler, allowing family members to live fuller lives along whatever paths they choose.

Chapter 8

Retirement:

When and How?

These days retirement planning is a major focus of people's investment planning. It should be: average life expectancy in Canada continues to rise, so people need to plan for a retirement that lasts much longer than was the case only a generation ago.

According to the latest information available through Statistics Canada, average life expectancy at birth is now more than eighty years. StatCan tells us that if you were a sixty-five-year-old man in the 2005 to 2007 period you can expect to live to eighty-three, and if you were a sixty-five-year-old woman you can expect to live to eighty-six.
Retirement means different things to different people. The secret to a happy retirement seems to be careful planning—financial planning, certainly, but also planning what you are going to do with your new-found time.

There Must Be More to Life Than This

What is your vision of retirement?

It seems we are surrounded these days by retirement advertisements featuring fit and fabulous-looking fifty-somethings or impossibly young-looking sixty-somethings enjoying themselves on a beach or on a golf course or in some exotic foreign locale. It all looks very glamorous; they all look very happy.

The implied message, of course, is that the advertiser can put you in one of those pictures. It could be you silhouetted by that watercolour sunset over the ocean; it could be you enjoying that refreshing gin and tonic in the shade after eighteen holes in the sun; it could be you climbing that mountain or snapping those incredible pictures on a photo safari. It could be you doing all these things—every one of them—tomorrow and tomorrow and tomorrow. Days of endless leisure and enough money to enjoy it, every day for the rest of your life.

For some this is indeed the picture of an ideal retirement. Usually, though, it is their ideal picture before they retire, not necessarily after they've been retired for a while. Far too many people spend most of their working lives labouring at something they don't really like doing, and they look forward to retirement as a chance to "finally get some fun out of life." After a while, many find that just having fun isn't so much fun anymore.

The research is fairly conclusive on this topic. The people who enjoy their retirement years the most, and who enjoy the best health in retirement, are not the ones spending their time in pursuit of various forms of entertainment but those engaged in challenging and meaningful activities.

One of my clients, Peter M., a wiry, white-haired, energetic entrepreneur in his late fifties, has built three companies and sold two of them. He fits the stereotype of the successful entrepreneur to a T: he's active, animated, confident, and he loves to take charge in any situation. Peter is independently wealthy yet he has made the choice to continue running his third company. He told me once he has several friends who have retired and who now spend their winters in Florida, in the same community where he and his wife have a home. He said his friends are always after him to retire, too, and spend warmer, more comfortable winters with them. When I asked him whether he was considering it, he became even more animated than usual.

"Susan, you've got to be kidding," he said. "I thought you knew me better than that! I mean, sure, I love taking a break from winter every now and then; who doesn't? But just between you and me, every time I come back from Florida I say to Helen, 'Honey, there must be more to life than this.' I mean all they do is golf and play bridge. Don't get me wrong, I love golf and I love bridge, too. But please, after four days of loafing I'm ready to climb the walls."

Peter described his business as the perfect playground for him.

"I need to stay busy and keep doing things. In my business there's always something new to think about, new markets to break into, new products to develop. You ask me about retirement? All I can say is, 'You're looking at it!' I intend to work until I can't work any longer."

What Is My Real Name, and What Do I Really Do?

Peter may be an extreme case; not too many people consider their work a playground. But his insistence that he will work until he can no longer do so touches on a very sensitive issue people face as retirement age draws near. The heading above rephrased from the old TV show What's My Line?—may overstate the case a bit, but for many people work is a major source of their sense of identity. For many it comes down to "I am what I do." The idea of not working, while it may hold a certain allure as a well-deserved reward for a lifetime of labour, also makes people question who they will be after they get the gold watch.

This question of post-retirement identity engenders in some people nothing but anxiety and worry and avoidance of the issue and in others a determination to become involved in—or remain involved in—activities they can pursue throughout their retirement years.

Bob S. is an example of someone in the latter category. The twinkle in his green eyes, his ready smile, and the bounce in his step are all indications that he did things right. As Bob approached the big event, he felt comfortable that he and his wife had enough money to support them through a long and comfortable retirement. He thought a lot about what he got out of work besides a salary, and he identified three things that he saw as the most important aspects of his work life.

First, a sense of purpose. As a successful book publisher, he felt he was on a constant crusade to discover and promote talented Canadian writers, and he believed his work contributed to the cultural landscape of the country.

Second, social relationships. Bob is an extremely affable man, and he valued the relationships he had forged throughout his career. He knew he needed to maintain an active social life if he was going to be happy in retirement.

And third, an environment in which he was continuously exposed to new ideas and new ways of doing things. He could not even begin to estimate the number of manuscripts he had read over the years, both fiction and nonfiction, and how much he had learned in the process. And when it came to new ways of doing things, well, he had seen more than a few major revolutions in the technology of book production over the course of his career.

Before the big event itself, he and his wife began planning for this major change in their lives. Bob retired from the publishing industry fifteen years ago at age sixty-five. What has he done in the intervening years to maintain his sense of purpose, maintain social relationships, and continue to learn new things? The list is exhaustive, so I'll share just a few highlights.

He and his wife joined a seniors group at their condo. It is called Live and Learn, and together the twenty or so people in this group take two courses each year at Toronto's Ryerson University, which has the largest continuing education enrolment of any university in Ontario. Put a check mark next to Learn New Things and Maintain Social Relationships.

He started a book club, which included two colleagues from his publishing company, three from his seniors group, and three people in their thirties who also live in his condo. Two more check marks.

Through his church Bob became involved in an initiative that provides books to families living at or below the poverty level, and his connections in the publishing industry are obviously a major asset to that group. He also volunteers time to an agency that promotes adult literacy. Two check marks next to Sense of Purpose.

I could go on and on about how Bob and his wife have crafted a successful and happy retirement, keeping physically active (he still skis at eighty) and involved in their children's and grandchildren's lives. But I'll stop here with something Bob said to me not along ago that sums it all up:

"I tell you what, Susan—I don't know how I ever had time for work!"

Start with a Solid Financial Foothold: Show Me the Numbers

A retirement like the one Bob and his wife enjoy presupposes a solid financial foundation. After all, although he remains extremely active in many areas of his life, he no longer actively earns income. Which brings us to the nitty-gritty of investment planning for retirement.

You may be surprised at the number of people who can give a fairly detailed account of how they want to live in retirement but don't have a realistic idea of how much it will cost them. In retirement planning, my philosophy is always the same: tell me how much you have right now, let's work out a reasonable estimate of your expenses in retirement and how long you're going to live, and I'll show you the numbers.

I met with new clients several years ago, a middle-aged couple who were excited about the rather fabulous retirement they envisioned and rightfully proud of the amount of money they had put aside. The problem was that although they had accumulated several million dollars, they could not fund their anticipated retirement lifestyle without eating into their capital. They were crestfallen when I showed them the projections.

Whether your vision of retirement is one of relaxed leisure or intense activity, projections based on conservative assumptions about market movements, interest rates, and portfolios returns are the best way I know to determine the right time to retire and the type of lifestyle you can afford.

When Couples Don't See Eye to Eye

The couple I just mentioned, although disappointed that they needed to put off retirement for several more years, were nonetheless lucky in one way: they were in agreement about what they wanted their retirement to look like. This is not always the case.

In my discussions with couples about their retirement, I have seen every possible permutation: couples in which the man has been the sole breadwinner and the woman has focused on raising the children; couples who have both had professional careers throughout their lives; couples in which the woman has inherited a substantial amount of money; couples who keep their financial accounts separate; and those who own much of their wealth jointly with only their RRSPs held separately.

No matter which of these scenarios presents itself, I can never tell before our discussion whether the couple is in sync about what they want their retirement to look like. And rest assured, it is their retirement even if the woman has never worked outside the home, because it is time they will spend together in a new way.

Sometimes couples are on the same page and sometimes they are not. Sometimes the man complains that his wife wants a retirement lifestyle that will cost too much money while the wife counters that he's too tight-fisted. She may have issues with the fact that the only money that is hers in her own right is her spousal RRSP. She may be ready to retire early and he may want her to continue working until he's ready or vice versa. Or she may want him to retire early and fund their retirement with her inheritance while he loves his work and wants to keep at it.

You never know what issues they may have, but whatever they are, they need to be reconciled before any appropriate retirement planning can be done.

I said emphatically at the start of chapter 1 that I am not a life coach, and I will reiterate that here. However, I have worked out a process that helps couples resolve differences about retirement. If they are both involved in the decision making—and when it comes to retirement planning both of them usually are involved—I have found that the best approach is to sit down with them and have a general discussion about their vision of retirement. It is here that differences often emerge.

Then I walk them through their Financial Scorecards individually, but in the presence of the other, this time with reference specifically to retirement. I do this with both spouses present because sometimes one person's answers come as a surprise to the other, and it helps for them to hear these surprises in a facilitated environment.

Then the three of us talk over the points of divergence in their Financial Scorecards. The rest is up to them. With each of their Scorecard issues clearly articulated and in writing, they have much better grounds for a mutually satisfying compromise.

If their financial assets are jointly held, it is absolutely essential that they articulate clear financial goals about retirement so we can be sure their investments appropriately reflect their wishes. Even when we manage separate accounts for them, it is much more efficient if we have a clear, unifying mandate against which we can weigh investment options. In my experience, a couple's success in defining and refining a common vision of retirement is a pretty good indicator of how successful their actual retirement together will be.

Chapter 9

You and Your Advisor:

Are You in the Right Relationship?

How did you choose your current advisor, and how satisfactory is the relationship? These questions are worth thinking about because working with the right advisor can be a key element in achieving your long-term financial goals.

In 2009, in the aftermath of the subprime meltdown and in the midst of market chaos and economic recession, an Ipsos Reid poll found that 87% of Canadian investors said they expected to be with their current advisor in a year's time. At first blush you would be justified in thinking this means there are an awful lot of people who are very well satisfied with their advisors. But is that what it means?

Obviously, the 13% who did not expect to be with their advisors in a year fall into the unsatisfied camp. The question is, how many of the 87% were truly satisfied, and how many were suffering from inertia, staying with their advisor simply because they were already with him or her? There is no way to tell because the poll did not ask that question.

In my practice, though, I have encountered innumerable people who actually waited until their advisor retired or moved to a different firm before seeking a new one, not because they were happy with the relationship but because they did not know how to extricate themselves from it. Sometimes there were family reasons for their inability to act: the advisor was a cousin or an aunt or a brother-in-law. Sometimes they failed to act out of sheer politeness; one woman told me she had stayed with her advisor so long simply because she did not want to hurt the advisor's feelings by taking her investments elsewhere. And sometimes they just had no idea how to go about finding an advisor who would be right for them.

A quick survey of the financial press in any given year will turn up dozens of articles about how important the advisory relationship is. The articles that go on to offer advice about how to find the right advisor usually include a list of questions investors should ask a prospective advisor. These articles underscore the fact that investors should actively interview advisors about how they operate and not simply listen to a sales pitch. They help put the investor in the driver's seat, which is exactly where they should be.

I like to think of this process as similar to what you would do if you were told you needed brain surgery. Would you be likely to allow just any surgeon to operate on you? Probably not. If you are at all like me, you would do your best to get all the information you could about the surgeons in your area who do the kind of surgery you need. You would want to know their reputations, where they were trained, how long they have been performing the particular procedure, how often they have performed it, and how often they perform it each day or week or month. You would want to know not just the success rate for this procedure in the general population but also what it is for each individual surgeon. And if you could not find a surgeon in your area whose qualifications satisfied you, you would go where you could find the right one.

My Wealth Advisor Selector™

Although a list of questions can be a great service to investors, how great it is depends entirely on the actual questions. I have found that not all lists are created equal. As a result I have created a tool called My Wealth Advisor Selector™ to help people when they are interviewing advisors. My Wealth Advisor Selector™ includes eight key questions that every investor should ask. As we did with Your Financial Scorecard, let's take a look at some of those questions to see why they are so important. This will give you a feel for how to interview prospective advisors if you decide to do so.

Q: What specific qualifications and experience do you have?

There may have been a time—long, long ago—when it was enough for a broker to have a keen market sense and be connected to a network of other market-savvy brokers for a constant flow of information and investment ideas. There may have been such a time, but if there was, it is now the fond memory of a handful of long-retired members of the old boys' club. Today's investment environment demands much more of advisors.

It demands a level of education that was almost unheard of a generation ago when the primary advisory model was transaction-based. Thanks in part to the emergence and pervasive influence of financial planning, the premier advisory model today is life-based, as we have discussed, and takes into consideration many aspects of a person's life, including their short- and long-term financial and personal goals.

Along with the evolution from transaction-based advisory to life-based advisory, advisors' responsibilities have also evolved, and they now need to develop a more comprehensive skill set. An advisor's professional designations is a good indication of how seriously they are taking that responsibility.

Let's face it, life is more complex today for many people than it was when June and Ward Cleaver and Beaver and Wally represented the ideal of North American living. Many investment products are also more complex and it seems new ones are being created every time you turn around. This means advisors must be committed to ongoing education if they are to understand these sophisticated securities and know when and how to use them properly.

At time of writing this book, the Investment Industry Regulatory Organization of Canada is developing the AdvisorReport which will provide investors with an online report regarding an Investment Advisor's employment history with IRROC Member firms; current approval categories; provinces where the individual is registered; educational background including industry courses completed for proficiency requirements; any terms and conditions on approval/registration and any past disciplinary record.

Personal lives are also more complicated; in many families both parents work outside the home, which creates both new opportunities and new stresses. In addition, many nontraditional family configurations have emerged in the last few decades, including families headed by gay couples. People are living longer, which means retirement now requires much more intensive long-term planning than used to be the case. All these factors create new needs, and only those advisors who keep current will have the tools to meet them.

Just as in finding a brain surgeon, you have every right to know what an advisor's credentials are and how much experience an advisor has. After all, you are contemplating putting your financial well-being in this person's hands.

Q: What do you do that is different from what other advisors do, and why would that be a benefit to me as your client?

Some advisors may find it difficult to answer this question because they have not set out to consciously differentiate their service offering from the service offering of the mainstream. It should be fairly evident from their response whether they actually do offer a more comprehensive level of service or not.

It never hurts to be even more specific in your questioning if you're not satisfied with the initial answer you get. After all, you want to know how this advisor can make a real difference in the way they will handle your affairs. The investment industry, like so many other industries, has its own jargon. Investment professionals understand this terminology and use it as a kind of shorthand; it can be a problem, though, if they use it when speaking to someone outside the industry. If this happens to you, you should simply ask the advisor to rephrase their response "in plain English."

You might want to ask them, "Do you provide individually customized solutions?" You want to know, for instance, whether the advisor takes the time to construct and manage different portfolios for their clients based on the individual needs and goals, as opposed to slotting clients into portfolios that are the same for everyone with the same risk profile.

Ask what resources the advisor can access through their firm, such as tax, estate, risk management and insurance planning, and advice on charitable giving/strategic philanthropy. And if you are a business owner, you may want to know whether succession planning is among the services the advisor can provide.

Some investment advisors are proactive in working with a client's other key advisors, such as tax advisors and estate lawyers. Find out whether this advisor will actively seek information from your other advisors who can influence the optimal structure of your portfolio or the appropriate activity in it (tax-loss selling, for instance).

Q: What can I expect in terms of reporting and servicing?

Before signing on with an advisor you should understand and be comfortable with the amount of information you will receive about your investments, when you will receive it, and in what form you will receive it. Will the advisor schedule regular progress reviews with you to talk about the performance of your portfolio and to determine whether there have been any material changes in your needs or your circumstances, or will the onus fall on you to initiate this kind of communication?

• • •

*What about reporting? Can you request customized reporting that breaks down your holdings in the way you want, or is the investment firm's general statement the only option? Some investors have particular reporting needs. Will the reporting you receive meet your specific requirements? For instance, one of my clients needed to know on an ongoing basis exactly how much cash he had in his account. He asked us to adjust his statements to indicate the actual cash in his account, separate from short-term securities. We now do this for him as a matter of course. If you do have special reporting needs, then establish, when you are interviewing advisors, whether they and their firm can meet them.

Q: How do you charge, and what will your services cost me?

You have every right to know exactly how much an advisor's services are going to cost you. You would not buy a house or a car or even a suit without understanding how much you were going to have to pay, so why would you engage an investment advisor before you have a clear idea of the cost? It is a straightforward question, but you probably would be surprised at the number of investors I talk to who do not know how much they pay their advisor or the mechanisms through which the advisor receives remuneration. Many investors overlook the fact that fees are tax deductible when unbundled but not when embedded in an investment.

Any ethical advisor will be more than happy to explain how they get paid, whether it is through fees or commissions or a combination of the two. I would caution you to beware if you get an answer like, "Don't worry about fees. I get paid by the mutual fund companies." The implication here is that the services you're receiving are not actually costing you anything. If this happens to you, it would be a good time to remind yourself of that familiar adage, "There's no such thing as a free lunch."

• • •

Sometimes old sayings seem as though they are stale and out of date, but this one has traction. Its staying power comes from the fact that it says something that is fundamentally true. In fact, this adage has been referred to as the idea "at the core of economics," and the free-market economist Milton Friedman even chose it as the title of his 1975 book on economics.

So, yes, the advisor may be paid by the fund company, but you are paying the fund company's management fee. Did the advisor mention that to you? In addition, many funds charge a redemption fee if you redeem within a certain period after purchase. So be sure to ask both parts of the question: How do you charge? and What will your services cost me?

In the final analysis, you want to be sure your advisor's method of remuneration is transparent and that the cost to you is reasonable; that is, it should be competitive vis-à-vis industry norms, and it should reflect an array of services based specifically on your individual needs.

Changing Advisors: Short-Term Pain for Long-Term Gain

I hope this discussion has helped highlight some of the things you should know about how your advisor runs his or her business. Perhaps you are among the 87% of investors who are planning to be with their current advisor in a year's time because you are satisfied with the relationship. If so, congratulations to both you and your advisor. If you have not talked these things over with your current advisor, though, I encourage you to do so. Remember that other old adage, "Better late than never."

If, however, you are among those who are simply experiencing inertia, or if you are among the 13% who have already decided to change advisors, then it is probably even more important for you to be asking questions such as these. Regardless of which category you fall into, keep in mind that you always have the right to look for a second opinion about how your investment affairs are structured. It can be a valuable exercise, one that confirms you are in good hands or raises red flags about your financial well-being.

It is sometimes easy to decide you should change advisors. Sometimes the reasons for change are obvious: poor service, faulty advice, lack of performance. Sometimes it comes down to sheer neglect. You wonder why your advisor never calls you or why you can never seem to reach them when you call. Sometimes the reasons are less evident: a vague feeling of dissatisfaction or a general sense that things could be better. Perhaps it is the unease you feel when every time you call someone new answers the phone, indicating instability in the advisor's team. Either way, though, once the decision is made it is still very difficult for many people to tell their advisor they are going to move their assets to another advisor at another firm.

On one level it is an intellectual decision, but on another level it is an emotional one. Sometimes an investor has a long-standing relationship with their advisor and the thought of rupturing that relationship is an uncomfortable one. Sometimes the advisor is a close personal friend or a family member, which exacerbates the problem. It is quite common for feelings of obligation or guilt to spring up and make it difficult to initiate the conversation about changing.

So, what should you do? You may not be surprised when I suggest you start by asking yourself this question again: "Three years from now, what would have to have happened for me to look back and be happy about my progress?" Be honest with yourself about whether you believe your current advisor is the one who can help you achieve your three-year financial goals, your goals for your family, and your goals for your future.

If the answer is no, the most direct way to make the change once you have found a new advisor is to pick up the phone, explain your decision, thank the advisor for their guidance over the course of the relationship, and ask for their cooperation in transferring your accounts. If you have not had a close relationship with your advisor, then an e-mail or a letter would be an appropriate way to let them know of your decision.

Whichever way you choose, you are likely to feel a sense of relief that you have dealt with the issue directly and a sense of excitement at being able to proceed with your new plans. In the long run, your personal and financial goals will be easier to achieve in a comfortable business relationship with the right advisor.

Chapter 10

Last Words

But First … a Word About My Sponsor

In the final analysis, I see myself as an independent businesswoman. The nature of my business, however, requires the "sponsorship" of a company through which I can provide the products and services my clients need. This brief section, then, is about my sponsor.

You may recall I mentioned in chapter 1 that I have moved from one firm to another twice in my career. Both times I was motivated by a desire to provide a deeper level of service and support to my clients, and both times I performed due diligence to identify the firm that offered the best opportunity to do so. I realize, though, that I have not really given you a very clear idea of how Richardson GMP fulfills my requirements as the right place to be.

I have mentioned the Richardson family's long history of success in wealth management with firms that predate Richardson GMP: Richardson Securities of Canada, Richardson Greenshields, and Richardson Partners Financial (the firm I joined in 2004 and the immediate precursor to Richardson GMP). But I would be remiss if I did not say something also about the specific benefits the firm brings to me as a wealth advisor and, more to the point, the benefits it brings to you through me.

Richardson GMP came into being in November 2009 with the merger of Richardson Partners Financial Limited and GMP Private Client L.P. (GMP stands for Griffiths McBurney Partners, the former name of that firm.) These two firms had dominated the top two positions in the Investment Executive newspaper's Brokerage Report Card over the previous two years, earning high scores in many areas, including wealth-management solutions for high-net-worth clients, ethics, stability, technology, compliance, product offering, and innovative investments.

The management of both firms realized their strengths complemented each other. The fit seems obvious now: two firms at the top of the industry serving the same client base can do so more effectively by combining resources.

Safeguarding Your Wealth. As a wealth advisor, I am committed to preserving your assets and enhancing your wealth over time. Preservation of clients' wealth is also a primary focus of Richardson GMP, and the firm has taken steps to ensure that its clients' assets are well protected.

Specifically, in addition to being a member of the Canadian Investor Protection Fund, Richardson GMP holds a separate insurance policy with Lloyd's of London that effectively doubles the basic coverage provided by CIPF to $2 million per general account and separate account. This is what I mean when I say that we give more than lip service to the notion of commitment to our clients' well-being. This enhanced coverage is not required by industry regulators; it is a completely voluntary gesture on the part of the firm to enhance the security of client assets.

Expanded Capabilities and Independence. Through its relationship with GMP Capital Inc., Richardson GMP offers enhanced services in many areas, including investment banking, asset management, alternative investment opportunities, trading desk capabilities, and equity research. Offering my clients the advice and the products that are best suited to their individual circumstance has always been a cornerstone of my business philosophy; the combined resources of Richardson GMP fortify my ability to provide full, unbiased advice and a greater range of services to my clients.

In-House Wealth Planning Expertise. The needs of the very wealthy are different from the needs of other investors. Because their affairs tend to be more complex, they often require more sophisticated solutions. One of the tremendous benefits available through my firm is access to a team of professionals with experience in many areas of wealth planning. Our in-house wealth management group consists of lawyers, accountants, tax professionals, and estate planners. I call on these experts as needed for services related to all types of planning needs, including financial, tax, insurance, philanthropic, and business succession planning.

As a seasoned advisor, I believe that the merger of Richardson Partners Financial and GMP Private Client has resulted in the preeminent independent investment firm in Canada, offering an unsurpassed array of products and services to meet clients' needs.

And Finally, Last Words

As we come to the end of this book, I'd like to reiterate what I hope it achieves for you.

First of all, I hope that reading it has given you the impetus to reflect on your life, your wealth, and the connection between the two. I hope you see how you can use your wealth as an enabler, a resource that allows you to accomplish the goals that are most important in your life.

I trust you now have clearer perspective on do-it-yourself investing. The question is: Do you have the time, the temperament, and the talent to go it alone? Whether your answer is yes or no, I hope you understand a bit more about the different types of investment advisors and about the investment industry. You should have a pretty clear idea of the range of services available from different advisors.

Hopefully you also have a good idea of some of the tough questions you have a right to ask of anyone who wishes to manage your money. Questions about their qualifications, about what they do differently that will be of benefit to you, about how they will communicate with you and whether they can provide the type of reporting you want, and finally, about how much their services will cost you. If you have not asked these questions of your current advisor, I encourage you to do so. Their answers can lead to one of two outcomes: a strengthening of your relationship or a parting of ways as you look for someone else to manage your financial affairs.

I hope you see, too, that no matter what group you may fit into—whether you are a busy professional, a successful entrepreneur, the overseer of a family business, or a widow dealing with money for the first time—your investment needs are uniquely your own because they flow from your own unique goals. The same is true even if you are just at the start of your career and beginning to think seriously about how to establish a sound savings and investment program. You owe it to yourself and to those who depend on you to find an advisor who can provide advice and deliver products and services tailored specifically to your situation.

I said at the start of this book that it would explain how I help my clients articulate a clear vision of their life goals and how that vision affects the appropriate investment of their assets. In closing, then, let me say that I hope you will remember these two simple questions and take the time to answer them for yourself:

> *"If you were at the end of your life looking back to today, what would have to have happened in the interim for you to feel you've lived your life with no regrets"?*
>
> *And, "If we were having this conversation three years from today, what would have to have happened for you to feel happy about your progress?"*

Together these questions can be a powerful guide for you. They can help you determine your long-term goals—both financial and nonfinancial—and the steps to take in the short term to achieve them.

Acknowledgements

The impetus for me to write It's Not Just About the Money – The Whole-Life Approach to Wealth Management came from many people. I am sincerely grateful to all of them.

First and foremost, I thank the many wonderful clients of The Latremoille Group whose trust and confidence in my abilities have been a source of inspiration for me. The origins and forms of your wealth, your life goals and wealth management needs—these are the realities that constantly encourage me to focus on giving the best advice possible in a world awash with financial information and investment products.

Secondly, I thank the members of my team at The Latremoille Group—Anne O'Farrell, Jody Bent, Margery Roden, Tori Roberts and Anne Kim—who work tirelessly to provide individual and customized service to each client. I thank the Richardson family and our partners at GMP for creating Richardson GMP Limited, an independent firm whose primary goal is to meet the wealth management and wealth planning needs of affluent Canadian families. The creation of this firm is an achievement that is helping to transform the private-client wealth management industry in Canada.

I am appreciative of the many people, who have shared their expertise with me to bring this book to fruition —especially Arnold Gosewich, who has guided me in defining the book's purpose and message, and Tom Churchill, who has now worked with me so closely on this and two previous books, helping translate my ideas, stories, and insights into cohesive chapters.

Finally, I thank my children, Nicholas and Sarah, for enabling me to juggle the role of parent with my professional life and the pursuit of excellence.

It is my hope that this book will inform, educate, and inspire those in need of wealth management advice, adding to their knowledge and strengthening their resolve to reach their financial and life goals.

June 16, 2010

Testimonials

This is a fitting follow-up to Susan's first book, The RichLife. That book showed what kind of person Susan is; this one shows what kind of wealth advisor she is—professional, prudent, and tenacious in pursuing her clients' best interests. C.M.

Susan knows people and she knows wealth management. In this book she shows how her proprietary process builds on this knowledge to produce investment results that support her clients' most cherished life goals. T.L.

In any field of endeavour, there are always a few who stand out from the crowd. Susan's depth of experience, practical investment knowledge, and attention to every detail of client service make her one of these. Managing the affairs of the wealthy requires a unique perspective and specialized skills, and Susan has both—this book shows how it should be done. D.S.

Susan guided us through the technology meltdown and the recent credit crisis, convincing us not to sell even though we were terrified. Now we can retire six months earlier than we had planned even while many of our friends are wondering if they can ever afford to retire. This book outlines Susan's approach to wealth management and gives you a glimpse into the heart and mind of a remarkable investment advisor. L.R.

I've had several financial advisors in my life, and I can say without hesitation that I do not plan to have another. Susan Latremoille and her team have figured out how to combine responsible investment management with unparalleled service and support. If you have the slightest—and I mean the slightest—concern about how your money is being managed, read this book now! A.B.

I highly recommend this book to anyone who wants to figure out how to get more from their money and more from their life. Susan approaches wealth management with knowledge, insight, and real personal warmth, and her clients benefit from all three. K.S.

NOTES: